MW01259824

conchs, tibias,
and harps

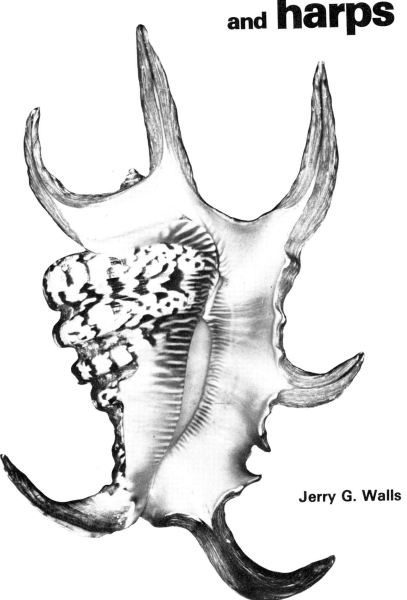

Jerry G. Walls

With thanks to Dr. R. Tucker Abbott, whose revisions of the conchs made a general work like this possible.

Front cover: Living *Strombus vomer hawaiensis*. Photo by Scott Johnson.

Back cover: Australian conchs. Photo by K. Gillett from *The Australian Great Barrier Reef in Color*.

Title page: *Lambis chiragra*. Photo by Walter Deas.

All photos by the author unless otherwise credited.

ISBN 0-87666-629-2

© 1980 T.F.H Publications Inc. Ltd.

Distributed in the U.S. by T.F.H. Publications, Inc., 211 West Sylvania Avenue, PO Box 427, Neptune, NJ 07753; in England by T.F.H. (Gt. Britain) Ltd., 13 Nutley Lane, Reigate, Surrey; in Canada to the book store and library trade by Beaverbooks Ltd., 150 Lesmill Road, Don Mills, Ontario M38 2T5, Canada; in Canada to the pet trade by Rolf C. Hagen Ltd., 3225 Sartelon Street, Montreal 382, Quebec; in Southeast Asia by Y.W. Ong, 9 Lorong 36 Geylang, Singapore 14; in Australia and the South Pacific by Pet Imports Pty. Ltd., P.O. Box 149, Brookvale 2100, N.S.W. Australia; in South Africa by Valid Agencies, P.O. Box 51901, Randburg 2125 South Africa. Published by T.F.H. Publications, Inc., Ltd, the British Crown Colony of Hong Kong.

Contents

Acknowledgments

Although the conchs and harps are small families, it has not been easy to assemble a complete collection for comparative and photographic purposes. Without the help of many people some essential species would have had to be omitted.

As in the previous books of this series, dealers have been of immense help. Bob and Dottie Janowsky of Mal de Mer Ent., Brooklyn; Dick Kurz of Wauwatosa, Wisc.; and Bob Morrison of Morrison Galleries, Sarasota, were all very helpful as usual and provided many specimens and contacts. M. Marescot of Tahiti provided excellent specimens from his area and Easter Island. Other material or photos were donated by Phillip Clover, Joel Greene, Colleen Jameson, Stan Jazwinski, Rodney Jonklaas, Jo' Kotora, Harry Lee, and Dot Schneider.

Russ Jensen of the Delaware Museum loaned several important specimens from his personal collection, and the staff of the museum were as generous and helpful as usual.

Warren E. Burgess read the manuscript and made valuable suggestions. Finally, Jim Bateman unstintingly loaned me specimens and gave advice. Often the opinions of an amateur are as valuable as those of an expert, especially when the amateur really enjoys and appreciates his shells.

Introduction

The two rather small families of molluscs included in this book have little in common other than their degree of popularity and the ease with which their families can be recognized. Both the Strombidae and the Harpidae have distinctive shell forms which cannot easily be confused with any other families, and the relatively few species of each family (about 72 conchs and 10 harps) have long been popular with shell collectors. Yet both families, although recently reviewed, still lack a good general treatment usable by collectors and readily available in book form. It is hoped that this book will adequately supply hobbyists with the photos and notes they need for the accurate identification of often similar and confusing species.

I have tried to illustrate a rather typical specimen of each species and subspecies of both families, but I have not tried to illustrate specimens in exceptionally nice condition. In many cases conchs are flawed shells, and such specimens have often been used for the photos. My rationale here is that the typical collector will probably never see truly gem specimens of such species as *Strombus gigas*, *S. galeatus*, or even *S. pipus*, so specimens in the normally collected condition have been illustrated. Although true gems of virtually all species do exist, in many cases they are high-premium shells and not available to all collectors.

In order to keep the size of the book small, usually only one or two specimens of each species or subspecies have been illustrated. All conchs and harps are variable, often extremely so. Virtually all conchs come in dark and light phases, there may be sexual dimorphism, and albinistic individuals are not uncommon. Harps vary greatly in intensity of pattern and details of rib and spire structure. No attempt has been made to illustrate such variants, but most collectors are aware of their existence and such variants should present no problems. Additionally, the specific characters in both conchs and harps are mostly those of structure, shape, or color that do not vary greatly from specimen to specimen or among populations.

The notes accompanying the photos attempt to give a brief description of the taxon and to mention, where necessary, characters that distinguish it from related taxa. The format varies slightly from subgenus to subgenus within *Strombus* and among the other genera so as to emphasize distinctive traits. The ranges are very general statements taken mostly from the literature, while the sizes given are almost certainly not the currently accepted maxima and minima. Anything said in the notes should be taken as a generalization; see the selected bibliography for revisions with more detailed descriptions. The arrangement of the photos within subgenera is generally alphabetical except when it was necessary to keep subspecies together on one page. Then a species might be shifted slightly in order.

It is hoped that this book will make collectors more aware of the conchs and harps as collectible shells. Although the popularity of the two families is already high, they are certainly not as popular as their beauty and variability deserve. Part of the problem has been that some conchs and harps are very poorly known and consequently difficult to identify. Some species are unfigured and so confusingly described in the literature available to collectors as to be unrecognizable. Perhaps with all the species figured and briefly described under one cover the interest in collecting conchs and harps will increase.

Family Strombidae

Conchs, spider conchs, tibias and terebellums are all members of the family Strombidae, one of three or four families comprising the superfamily Strombacea. This superfamily is rather closely related to the cowry superfamily Cypraeacea and has a similar radula, reproductive system and feeding behavior (see Walls, 1979). All are herbivorous, feeding on algal and detrital films on plants and stones by grazing. Unlike the cowries, the mantle is small and does not cover the dorsum of the shell; the aperture may have one or both lips toothed, but the body whorl does not inflate to "swallow" the spire.

CONCH ALLIES

Two very closely related families of Strombacea are the Aporrhaidae (pelican's-foot shells) and the Struthiolariidae (ostrich's-foot shells or struths). These two families are more typical of colder water than most conchs, with the first family found from the northern Atlantic to South Africa and the second from cold waters of the Australia - New Zealand - Antarctic area. Pelican's-feet are very similar to small *Lambis* at first glance as they have three or more long projecting digits on the outer lip and a long anterior canal. The species are usually heavily sculptured with small knobs on the spire and body whorl and often have heavy axial and spiral ridges as well. The shells are plain brown, seldom with a strong pattern. The exact species count is uncertain because of confusion with fossil species and bothersomely indistinct species boundaries in living material, but it seems that all the living species can be assigned to the genus *Aporrhais* without difficulty. Most species are West African and Mediterranean in distribution, with one species found on the northern North American coast. About five species are currently sold by dealers, but other species or varieties are sometimes available. *Aporrhais pespelicani* is the most common species.

Struths look very much like squat, rather inflated conchs. The body whorl is large and rounded; the mouth is also large and usually with strong calluses, and there may be a shallow stromboid notch in some species. The spire is turreted and usually nodulose. Color patterns are typically brown on brown as in most cold-water shells. The number of living species is again uncertain, but at least three species of the genus *Struthiolaria* are commonly available to collectors; these are all Australian and New Zealand species, but there are additional species found closer to the Antarctic continent. Both pelican's-feet and struths are of very secondary collector importance, are poorly known taxonomically, and are not easily available for review, so they are not discussed in detail.

Sometimes included in the Strombacea is the Xenophoridae or carrier shells. These rounded, depressed shells (mostly of the genus *Xenophora*) are superficially like turbinids *(Turbo, Calliostoma,* etc.*)* in shape but differ from them anatomically. Lately their classification has varied from author to author, but certainly they are not superficially similar enough to be considered related to conchs by collectors. The two-score species are collectable, but they are seldom of interest to conch collectors.

CONCHS

The family Strombidae contains forms that are variable in shape and sculpture, although most genera and species are readily recognizable as conchs by the presence of the "stromboid notch" at the anterior part of the outer lip. This usually shallow notch is thought to serve as a "peek-hole" for the right eye of the conch. Commonly the anterior canal is long, the spire is conical and often with varices or growth thickenings, and the columellar callus is thick and strongly developed. There are often teeth or lirae (ridges) developed on the columellar callus and within the mouth. The spire and body whorl are often heavily sculptured with ridges and knobs, but in many species the entire shell is practically smooth. Digits sometimes are found on the outer lip, and there may be a strongly developed posterior canal as well. Experience with a few species of conch will readily allow collectors to recognize almost any species as belonging to the family.

Anatomically conchs and their allies are not highly modified. The long and muscular proboscis gathers food for rasping by the radular teeth. These teeth are of three types: (1) a rectangular cen-

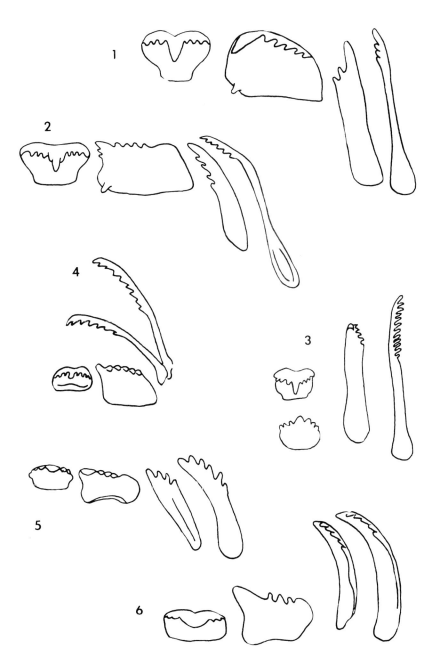

Representative conch radular teeth (after Abbott): 1) *Strombus canarium;* 2) *Strombus epidromis;* 3) *Strombus gibberulus;* 4) *Terebellum terebellum;* 5) *Lambis lambis;* 6) *Lambis truncata.*

9

tral tooth, flanked by a rather similar (2) lateral tooth on each side, then by one or two slender, elongated, often curved (3) marginal teeth. Each type of tooth bears distinct denticles or cusps that are variable at the generic, subgeneric, and often specific level. The gut passes over the radular cavity to become the stomach and then the intestine, rectum and anus. The siphon is another major part of the anterior anatomy. Often shielded by the elongated anterior (siphonal) canal, it is a projection of the mantle folded to allow water to circulate over the long series of gills (ctenidia.) At the base of the proboscis are the two usually greatly elongated eyestalks that end in large, round button-like eyes often with startling patterns of blue or yellow rings around a black central area. The eyestalks are often actively moving, apparently scanning the area for enemies. In most conchs the right eyestalk is somewhat to much shorter than the left, perhaps related to the presence of the stromboid notch on the outer lip at the right margin of the shell. Extending beyond the eyestalks are often very long and narrow pointed tentacles that are presumably either sensory in function or serve to help protect the eyes.

The foot in most conchs is large, pointed, powerful, and with a large to small curved and serrated operculum at the hind end. The

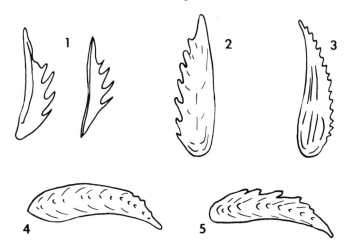

Representative conch opercula (after Abbott): 1) *Terebellum terebellum*; 2) *Strombus helli*; 3) *Strombus epidromis*; 4) *Strombus lentiginosus*; 5) *Strombus decorus*.

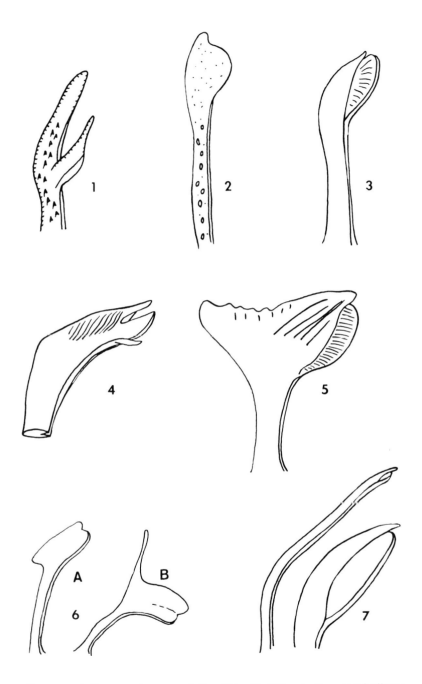

Representative conch verges (after Abbott): 1)*Terebellum terebellum;*
2) *Strombus taurus;* 3) *Strombus helli;* 4) *Strombus epidromis;* 5)
Strombus plicatus; 6a) *Strombus gibberulus gibbosus;* 6b) *Strombus
gibberulus gibberulus;* 7) *Lambis lambis.*

operculum is usually thickened on one margin and has the serrations of the other margin variable from small and rather indistinct to very large and few in number. There seems to be a correlation between the species and the number and form of serrations, but this has never been investigated in detail. Seldom does the operculum fill the entire aperture, although in some *Tibia* species and in *Strombus gigas* it may be very large.

Sexual dimorphism is sometimes prominent in conchs, with females often much larger and broader than males. In *Lambis* there are also obvious differences in the curvature of the digits and the shape and positioning of the larger dorsal knobs. Males of all strombids have a large penis or verge on the right dorsal part of the body, this penis bearing an open groove and often ending in a distinctly forked or ax-shaped head. The exact shape of the penis is often used as a supplemental subgeneric and even specific character in *Strombus,* but it is of course not practical for use by the vast majority of collectors.

DEVELOPMENT

Conchs have the sexes separate, as mentioned, and usually pair for mating, although as many as three or four males have been noticed associated with a spawning female. The eggs, usually at least 100,000 to 500,000 in number, are very small and covered by a thick rounded jelly sheath. They are contained within a narrow tube of jelly that forms a coiled mass coated with sand particles. When unraveled the egg string may exceed 50 feet in length. Spawning females commonly hold the egg mass under the lip of their shell for the four or five days it takes for the eggs to hatch.

The free-swimming veliger larvae of conchs (specifically *Strombus*) have a well-developed velum or swimming fold that varies from a two-lobed structure in recently hatched larvae to a many-lobed one in older larvae. The larvae at first feed on microscopic planktonic algae, but as they grow they begin to take larger algae and finally algal film from off the surface. The larval stage lasts about two or three weeks in the few species where the life cycle has been properly studied, after which time the larvae settle to the bottom and begin to metamorphose into the juvenile stage. This period of change lasts about one or two weeks before the juvenile

Right: Dorsal view of newly metamorphosed *Strombus gigas* at 29 days of age (after Brownell). Below: Juvenile shells of three common Caribbean conchs. From left to right: *Strombus gigas,* 31.5mm; *Strombus pugilis,* 36.5mm; *Strombus costatus,* 33.5mm (after Brownell).

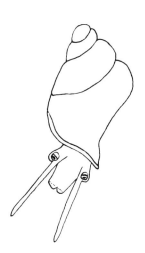

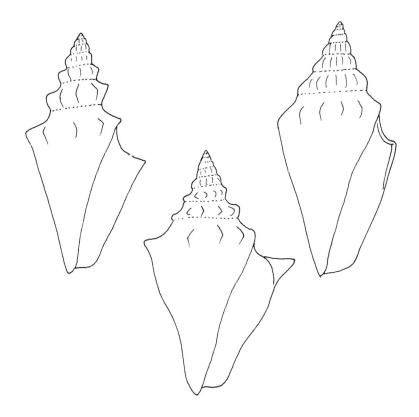

is fully developed. Juveniles and metamorphosing individuals feed on algal films off the substrate, a feeding procedure retained in the adult. The life span of conchs is unknown, but the larger species can live to at least three years, while the smaller species have presumably shorter life spans.

The shells of juvenile conchs are often quite different from those of the adults, but the juvenile sculpture is usually preserved on the early whorls of the adult shell. Varices or thickenings occur in most young conchs, presumably as a method of strengthening the shell to discourage the many predatory animals that prey on small conchs (crabs, hermit crabs, fishes, octopuses, and many molluscs, including in a few recorded cases other conchs). The rate of growth of the juvenile varies with species and food availability, but it is presumably quite rapid. Subadults have the normal adult shell characters, although often poorly developed. Thus the spines and knobs may be weak or almost absent even in large subadults or juveniles, and commonly the outer lip is not completely thickened until full maturity is reached. The coloration of juveniles and subadults may be similar to that of the adult, but in species with deeply colored mouths the full coloration is also not reached until maturity. In some species an aluminum-colored glaze develops on the columella and lip of very large adults.

ECOLOGY

As mentioned, all adult conchs (as far as is known) are herbivorous, feeding on algae, detritus, and in some cases higher marine plants such as sea grasses; they rarely eat animal matter, though cases of cannibalism have been noted. They are thus of prime ecological importance in some shallow-water food chains. In many parts of the world the larger and medium-sized species of *Strombus* are regularly taken as food and are important commercially. In the Caribbean the queen conch, *Strombus gigas,* is fished so heavily that in many areas it is rapidly becoming uncommon or even rare. Large conchs probably have relatively few enemies because of the thickened shell, although the large aperture makes them easier prey than would be thought. The small conchs,

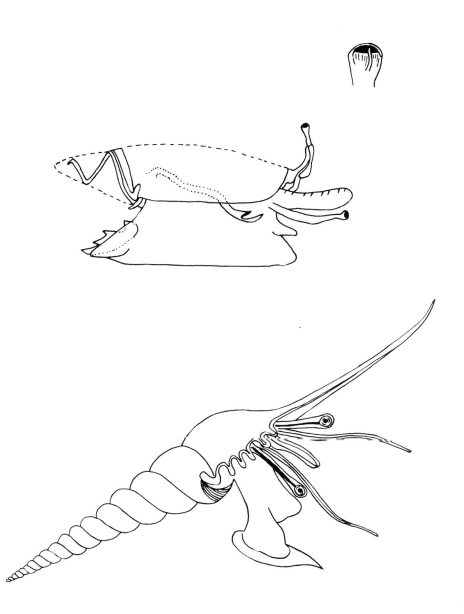

Diagrammatic views of the living animals of *Terebellum terebellum* above (with detail of eye showing short tentacle) and *Tibia fusus* below. *Terebellum* after Jung and Abbott; *Tibia* after Abrea (*HSN* 23(6), 1975).

however, are heavily preyed upon by many molluscs, crustaceans, and fishes.

The Strombidae is an old family with many described fossil members. Today the family is well represented only in the Indo-Pacific, with no species in the Mediterranean, one species in western Africa, and a few species on each coast of the Americas. Conchs are mostly tropical animals of shallow waters, which is in keeping with their herbivorous habits. Although Caribbean species extend north on offshore reefs to the Carolinas and *Strombus maculatus* occurs south to Easter Island, the other species are more typical of warmer waters from the Ryukyus to Mozambique, Queensland, and Tahiti.

There are several deep-water conchs, specifically the tibias and *Strombus listeri;* several other *Strombus* (such as *S. kleckhamae* and *S. plicatus sibbaldi*) may be deep-water but are poorly known. Since these species occur below the zone of plant growth, they are presumably detritus feeders that burrow in the bottom. In at least some cases this burrowing behavior is correlated with an elongated anterior canal.

Terebellum is a shallow-water strombid that burrows in sand and presumably feeds on detritus; in this genus the tentacles are very short, presumably because the eyes are kept at the surface of the sand and do not need extra protection or detectors.

THE MAPS

The following range maps for the Strombidae and Harpidae are intended as visual aids in understanding the distribution of living conchs and harps. Most are generalized and updated versions of similar maps presented by Abbott in papers cited in the bibliography. Gaps between segments of a species' range are in most instances probably due more to an absence of collectors than to an absence of animals, although the ranges of several species appear to be shrinking to some extent. Fossil occurrences are not considered in these maps. The ranges of subspecies are seldom as sharply defined as shown, with the usual situation being a relatively broad zone of intergradation where the subspecies are in proximity. This should be remembered when using the maps.

FAMILY STROMBIDAE

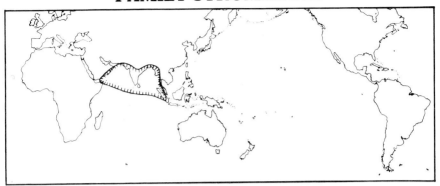

MAP 1. Distribution of *Tibia (Tibia) delicatula.*

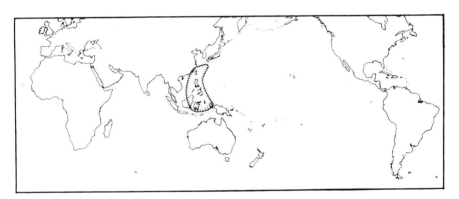

MAP 2 Distribution of *Tibia (Tibia) fusus.*

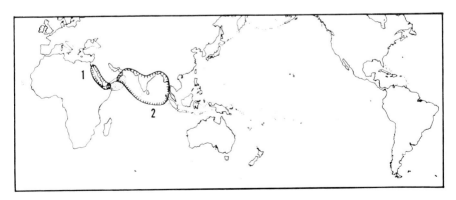

MAP 3. Distribution of *Tibia (Tibia) insulaechorab:* 1) *T. i. in-sulaechorab;* 2) *T. i. curta;* stipple = intergradation.

17

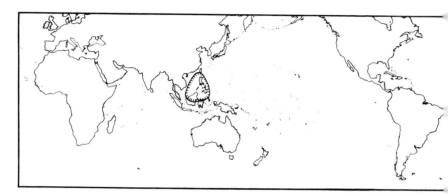

MAP 4. Distribution of *Tibia (Tibia) martini.*

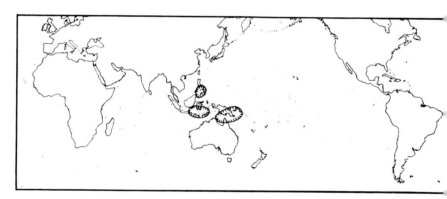

MAP 5. Distribution of *Tibia (Rimella) cancellata.*

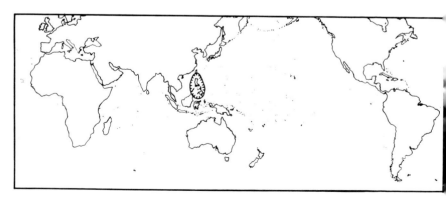

MAP 6. Distribution of *Tibia (Rimella) crispata.*

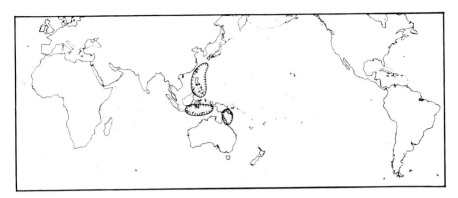

MAP 7. Distribution of *Tibia (Rimella) powisi.*

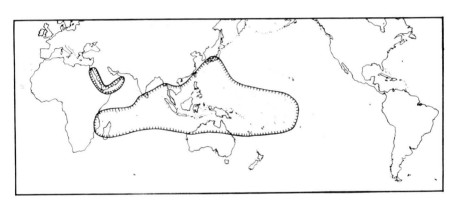

MAP 8. Distribution of *Terebellum torebellum.*

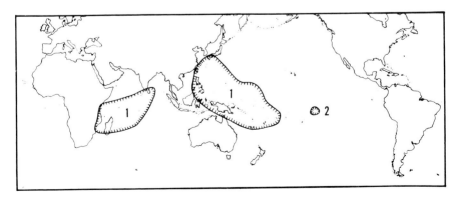

MAP 9. Distribution of *Lambis (Lambis) crocata:* 1) *L. c. crocata;* 2) *L. c. pilsbryi.*

19

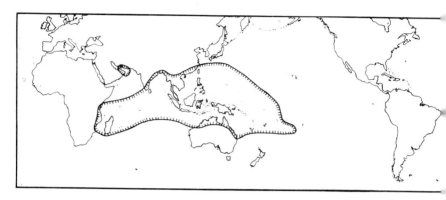

MAP 10. Distribution of *Lambis (Lambis) lambis.*

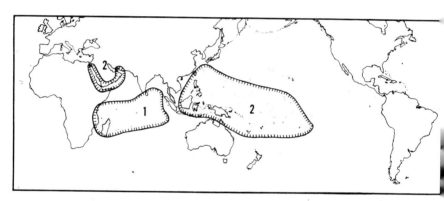

MAP 11. Distribution of *Lambis (Lambis) truncata:* 1) *L. t. truncata;* 2) *L. t. sebae.*

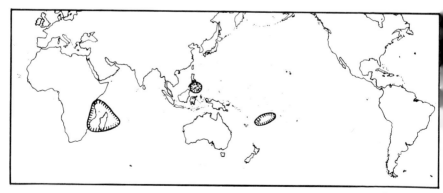

MAP 12. Distribution of *Lambis (Millepes) digitata.*

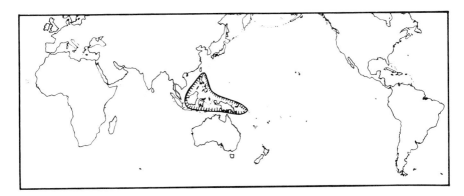

MAP 13. Distribution of *Lambis (Millepes) millepeda.*

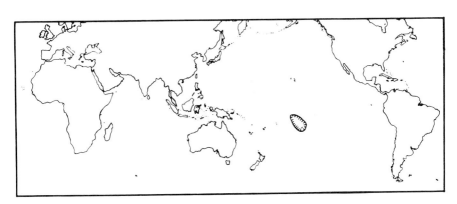

MAP 14. Distribution of *Lambis (Millepes) robusta.*

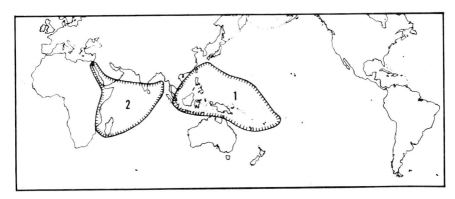

MAP 15. Distribution of *Lambis (Millepes) scorpius:* 1) *L. s. scorpius;* 2) *L. s. indomaris.*

21

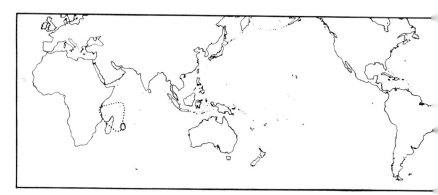

MAP 16. Distribution of *Lambis (Millepes) violacea* (dotted line indicates doubtful occurrences).

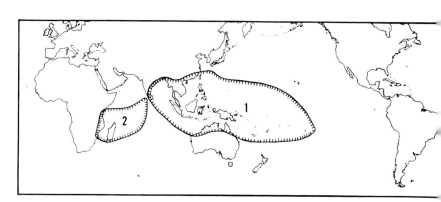

MAP 17. Distribution of *Lambis (Harpago) chiragra:* 1) *L. c. chiragra;* 2) *L. c. arthritica.*

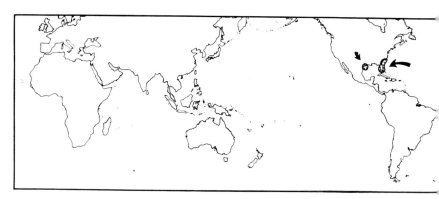

MAP 18. Distribution of *Strombus (Strombus) alatus.*

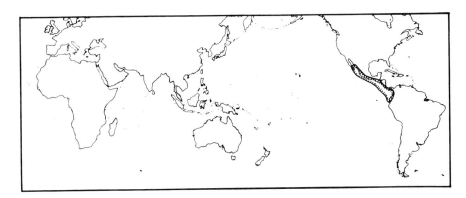

MAP 19. Distribution of *Strombus (Strombus) gracilior.*

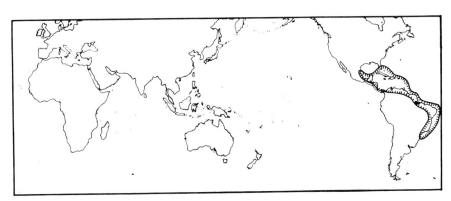

MAP 20. Distribution of *Strombus (Strombus) pugilis.*

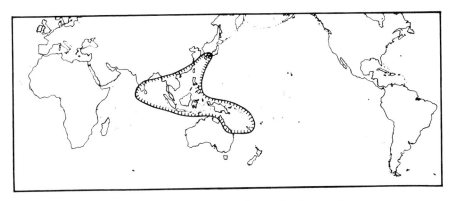

MAP 21. Distribution of *Strombus (Laevistrombus) canarium.*

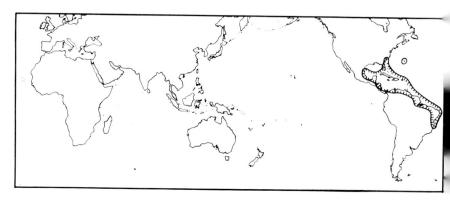

MAP 22. Distribution of *Strombus (Tricornis) costatus.*

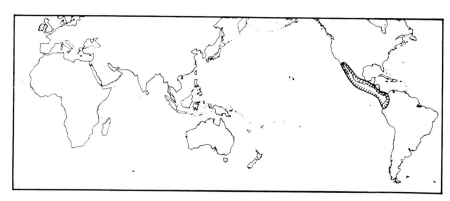

MAP 23. Distribution of *Strombus (Tricornis) galeatus.*

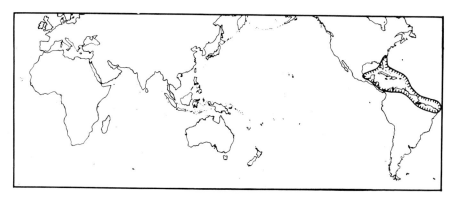

MAP 24. Distribution of *Strombus (Tricornis) gallus.*

24

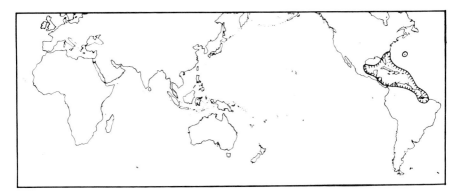

MAP 25. Distribution of *Strombus (Tricornis) gigas*.

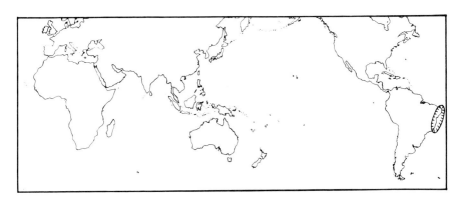

MAP 26. Distribution of *Strombus (Tricornis) goliath*.

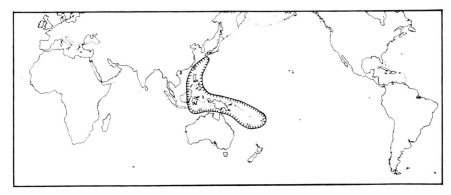

MAP 27. Distribution of *Strombus (Tricornis) latissimus*.

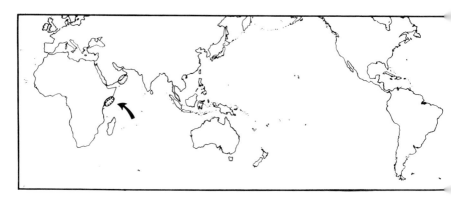

MAP 28. Distribution of *Strombus (Tricornis) oldi.*

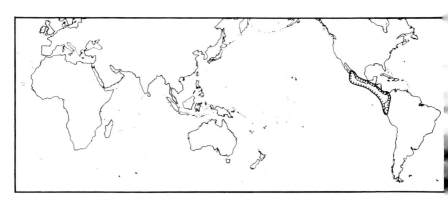

MAP 29. Distribution of *Strombus (Tricornis) peruvianus.*

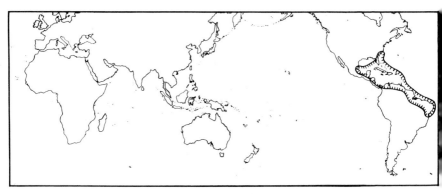

MAP 30. Distribution of *Strombus (Tricornis) raninus.*

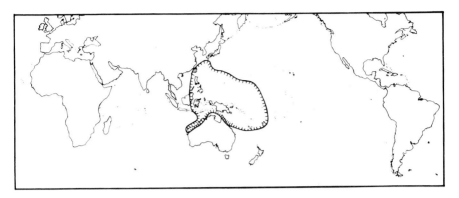

MAP 31. Distribution of *Strombus (Tricornis) sinuatus.*

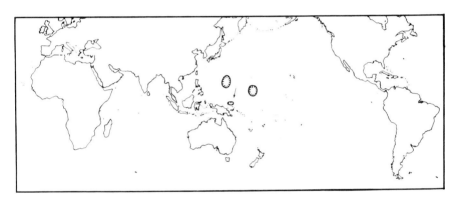

MAP 32. Distribution of *Strombus (Tricornis) taurus.*

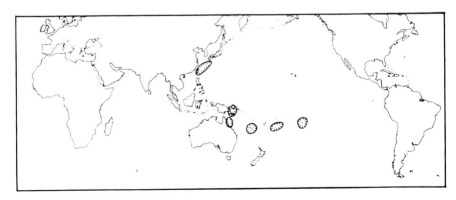

MAP 33. Distribution of *Strombus (Tricornis) thersites.*

27

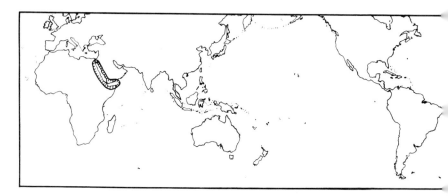

MAP 34. Distribution of *Strombus (Tricornis) tricornis.*

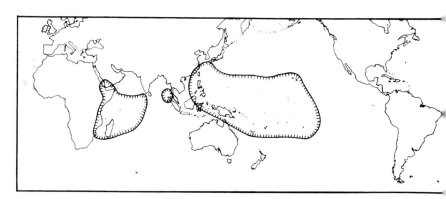

MAP 35. Distribution of *Strombus (Canarium) dentatus.*

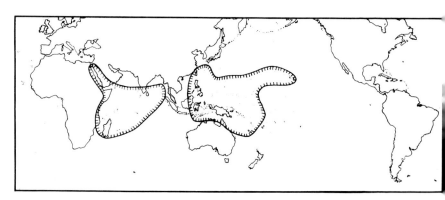

MAP 36. Distribution of *Strombus (Canarium) erythrinus.*

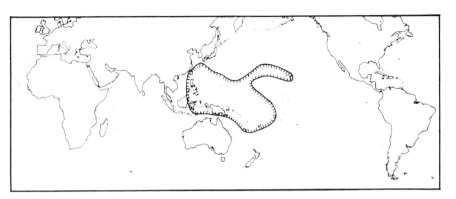

MAP 37. Distribution of *Strombus (Canarium) fragilis.*

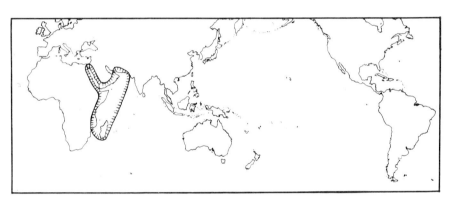

MAP 38. Distribution of *Strombus (Canarium) fusiformis.*

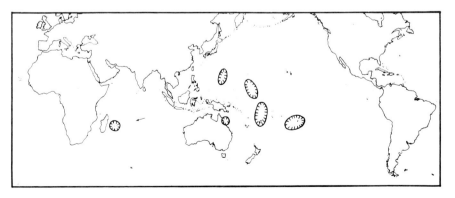

MAP 39. Distribution of *Strombus (Canarium) haemastoma.*

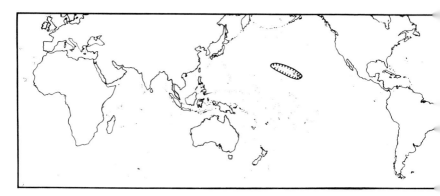

MAP 40. Distribution of *Strombus (Canarium) helli.*

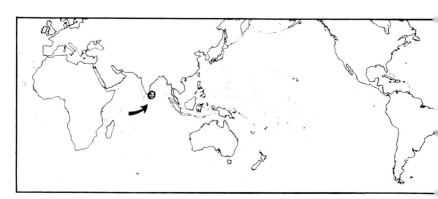

MAP 41. Distribution of *Strombus (Canarium) klineorum.*

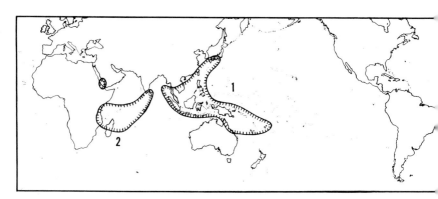

MAP 42. Distribution of *Strombus (Canarium) labiatus:* 1) *S. l. labiatus;* 2) *S. l. olydius.*

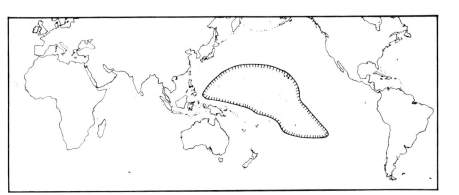

MAP 43. Distribution of *Strombus (Canarium) maculatus.*

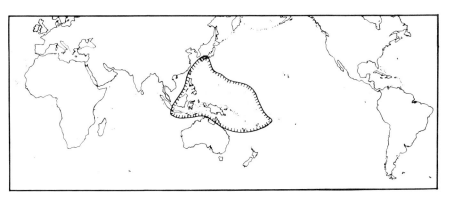

MAP 44. Distribution of *Strombus (Canarium) microurceus.*

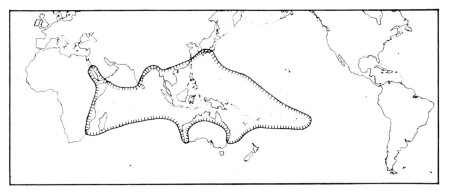

MAP 45. Distribution of *Strombus (Canarium) mutabilis.*

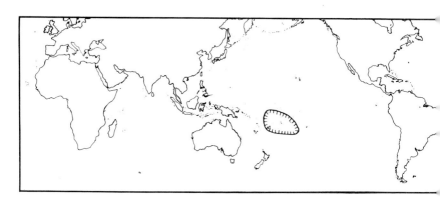

MAP 46. Distribution of *Strombus (Canarium) rugosus.*

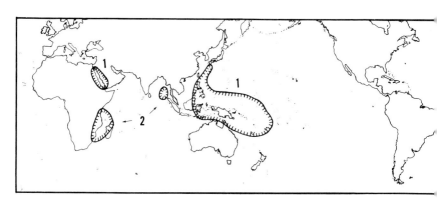

MAP 47. Distribution of *Strombus (Canarium) terebellatus:* 1) *S. t. terebellatus;* 2) *S. t. afrobellatus.*

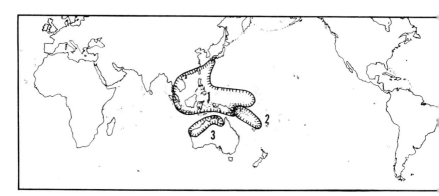

MAP 48. Distribution of *Strombus (Canarium) urceus:* 1) *S. u. urceus;* 2) *S. u. incisus;* 3) *S. u. orrae.*

32 (Maps continue on page 160

LAMBIS (MILLEPES) "WHEELWRIGHTI" Greene, 1978: Aperture and columella with lirae present, sometimes not very distinct on the columella; usually 7 digits, sometimes 8-9, plus the anterior canal, the first digit simple; spire partially covered with a heavy callus. Brownish dorsally; aperture creamy tan or orangish, often darker brown at the outer lip and on the columellar callus. 185-225mm total length. Rare; known only from the Philippines. Perhaps just a gigantic gerontic *L. millepeda* population, or more likely a hybrid between *L. millepeda* and *L. truncata*. Not considered a valid species, but listed here for future reference.

LAMBIS (MILLEPES) ROBUSTA (Swainson, 1821): Aperture and columella with very strong crowded lirae; 6 long, nearly smooth digits, the anterior ones hooked, the first simple and without a distinct lobe, the anterior canal long and curved. Aperture edged with orange or peach to tan, heavily covered with black and white streaks, as is the columella; no white bar in posterior part of aperture near the pit. Whitish above with brown axial stripes or blotches. Length 100-190mm. Uncommon or rare in French Polynesia and the Line Islands. This species is very similar to *L. scorpius* in appearance and pattern as well as sculpture, differing in the nearly smooth digits and the absence of a white bar in the aperture. Another very good character is the fact that the bases of digits 3 and 4 are very close together, almost fused, the fourth digit sometimes distinctly smaller than the fifth. The third and fourth digits are regularly spaced in *L. scorpius*.

Lambis "wheelwrighti" (= *L. millepeda* X *L. truncata?)*

Lambis (Millepes) robusta

ambis (Millepes) scorpius scorpius

ambis (Millepes) scorpius indomaris

LAMBIS (MILLEPES) SCORPIUS SCORPIUS (Linnaeus, 1758): Aperture and columella with very strong crowded whitish lirae; 6 long, nodulose digits, the anterior ones hooked, the first simple but usually with a distinct flap at its base; the anterior canal long, slender, and usually strongly curved. Edge of mouth often tan or bright orange, heavily streaked with black and white within, as is the columella; a distinct white bar within the posterior part of the aperture at the deep pit. Whitish or tan above with few to many brownish streaks and blotches. The typical subspecies is distinguished by the presence of a large lobe or flap at the base of the first digit. Length 95-170mm. It is common in the western Pacific east to the Samoan area.

LAMBIS (MILLEPES) SCORPIUS INDOMARIS Abbott, 1961: A very weakly differentiated subspecies distinguished from the nominate *L.s. scorpius* by the absence of a lobe at the base of the first digit or its reduction in size and folding over spire. Typically the anterior digits are shorter basally than in the other subspecies and dorsally are darker distally. These are all variable characters in large series and the subspecies is often difficult to recognize. Indian Ocean, where it is not uncommon.

LAMBIS (MILLEPES) VIOLACEA (Swainson, 1821): Aperture heavily lirate but columella often with only traces of lirae; 9-11 digits plus a short anterior canal, the anterior digits very short and the first (posterior) digit bifurcated; spire relatively low and wide, the last whorl with a very prominent margin. Mouth glossy white, dark violet or purple deep within, the columella usually white and stained with purple or deep pink; digits white beneath. Whitish above with brown blotches or spots, brighter reddish brown below with spiral or axial rows of white dots. Length 75-125mm. Rare, the most expensive spider conch; definitely known only from Mauritius, but often reported (incorrectly?) from Reunion and Madagascar. *L. digitata* also has a bifurcated first digit, but it differs in mouth color and having the digits brown beneath.

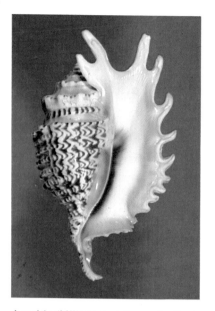 

Lambis (Millepes) violacea (both above and below)

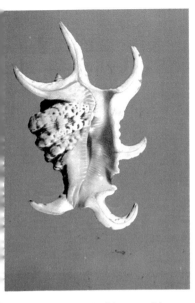

Lambis (Harpago) chiragra chiragra

Lambis (Harpago) chiragra arthritica

LAMBIS (HARPAGO) CHIRAGRA CHIRAGRA (Linnaeus, 1758): Very thick and heavy, the aperture and columella with low or strong lirations; 5 very thick digits, the first bent to the left and perpendicular to the body axis, the anterior canal large and parallel to the first digit; dorsum with 4-5 very heavy spiral ridges bearing low knobs. Tan to dark brown above with white spots on the ridges. In the typical subspecies the aperture is rosy, the columella paler, with the lirations very weak and colorless to very strong and streaked with black and white; there is a deep axial pit in the posterior part of the aperture. In the poorly understood form *rugosa* (Sowerby) the columella and sometimes aperture bear blackish lirae; this is usually a highly developed male, females having the dark lirae weak or indistinct. Adult females about 100-260mm long, males 95-150mm, sometimes smaller, variable with population. Common in the Pacific east to French Polynesia and in the eastern and northern Indian Ocean.

LAMBIS (HARPAGO) CHIRAGRA ARTHRITICA Roeding, 1798: Very similar in appearance to the *rugosa* form of the nominate subspecies, with heavy black and white lirae on the columella and usually in the aperture; the aperture is somewhat less rosy and more yellowish in color. The main distinction is that in *L.c. arthritica* the deep pit in the posterior part of the aperture just above the margins of the throat is absent. Adult size smaller, 120-190mm, with less distinct sexual dimorphism. Eastern Africa to the Maldives; apparently absent from the northwestern Indian Ocean.

STROMBUS (STROMBUS) ALATUS Gmelin, 1791: Heavy, with a moderate gloss. Body whorl nearly smooth; columella smooth except for a few faint lirae anteriorly and posteriorly; outer lip thickened, flared, the notch deep; weak lirae on outer lip near margin; outer posterior angle of lip rounded, not erect. Spire low to tall, penult whorl and shoulder with strong spines about equal in length or those of shoulder longer. Usually some shade of tan, mottled, often darker anteriorly; ventral surface with glossy tan, violet, or orange callus; aperture whitish, margined with tan, orange, violet, or black; anterior end of shell dark violet. Northeastern Gulf of Mexico, both coasts of Florida, Texas, and north to the Carolinas; a similar shell of uncertain status occurs in the Caribbean; common. Length 40-117mm. Very like *S. pugilis* and often with intermediates, but usually with a sloping angle of the lip and the shoulder spines not shorter than those of the penult whorl.

STROMBUS (STROMBUS) GRACILIOR Sowerby i, 1825: Heavy, with a good gloss. Body whorl nearly smooth, as is columella; outer lip thickened, flared, the notch deep; outer lip usually smooth; outer posterior angle rounded, slightly erect. Spire moderate to tall, with rounded marginal knobs; spiral ridges nearly absent on later whorls; penult whorl and shoulder with short, pointed spines, those of shoulder longer. Pale tan to bright orange, often with pale spiral bands at shoulder and midbody; ventral callus tan or orange, glossy; aperture bluish white, narrowly margined with reddish, anterior end violet. Eastern Pacific, Gulf of California to Ecuador; common. Length 40-95mm. The spines are shorter than in the Atlantic species and the spiral ridges on the later spire whorls are weak or absent.

Strombus (Strombus) alatus

Strombus (Strombus) gracilior

Strombus (Strombus) pugilis

Strombus (Laevistrombus) canarium

STROMBUS (STROMBUS) PUGILIS Linnaeus, 1758: Heavy, with a good gloss. Body whorl nearly smooth, as is columella; outer lip thickened, flared, the notch deep; outer posterior angle erect; margin of outer lip often with weak lirae. Spire low to tall, with strong spiral ridges and marginal knobs; penult whorl and shoulder with strong spines, those of penult whorl usually longer than those of shoulder (which may occasionally be absent or reduced). Usually some shade of yellowish or orange dorsally, sometimes with paler bands at shoulder and midbody; ventral callus glossy yellowish to red or tan; aperture whitish, broadly margined with orange to red, dark violet anteriorly. Southern Florida through the Caribbean and Central America to central Brazil; common. Length 25-100mm. Quite variable in color and spine development. The bright colors and erect angle of the lip are usually sufficient to tell it from *S. alatus,* but the penult spines being longer than the shoulder spines is also a good character.

STROMBUS (LAEVISTROMBUS) CANARIUM Linnaeus, 1758: Heavy, thick, with a good gloss. Body whorl nearly smooth, without spines, as is columella; outer lip thick, flared, smooth, the outer posterior edge erect to sloping; notch shallow. Spire tall to moderate, with weak spiral ridges and sometimes heavy varices. Brownish to grayish, often with network of fine closely spaced irregular axial brown lines; ventral surface with thick white callus; aperture and outer lip white. Specimens with relatively tall and narrow spires have been called var. *turturella* (Roeding) but are individual variants. Common in the western Pacific from Japan to New Hebrides and in the Indian Ocean from Malaysia to India. 35-100mm long. The simple sculpture and shape are distinctive.

STROMBUS (TRICORNIS) COSTATUS Gmelin, 1791: Very thick and heavy, with a good gloss. Body whorl with low and often indistinct spiral ridges dorsally, the columella smooth; outer lip thickened, flared, rounded posteriorly but low; notch rather shallow. Spire moderate, with weak marginal knobs that do not project greatly; shoulder with three or more heavy knobs. Dorsum tan to cream, only the spire with darker brown axial streaks; white ventrally, the callus thick and smooth; entire mouth white; whole shell rarely tinted pink or violet. Carolinas south through Caribbean to Brazil; common. 100-175mm long. The uniformly white mouth, relatively low posterior margin of the lip, and only weakly nodulose spire are distinctive.

STROMBUS (TRICORNIS) GALEATUS Swainson, 1823: Very thick and heavy, usually eroded. Body whorl with broad or narrow spiral ridges that may be visible ventrally in small shells; columella smooth; outer lip thickened, flared, rounded posteriorly but low; notch shallow. Spire moderate, pointed, without distinct nodules but usually very badly eroded; shoulder with very low and indistinct knobs. Tan to white above, similar below; columellar callus and margin of mouth often tinted with yellow or salmon; edge of lip sometimes with brown bars; aperture white. Eastern Pacific, Gulf of California to Ecuador; common. Length 150-230mm. *S. goliath* is rather similar but much larger, has the outer lip expanded posteriorly beyond the tip of the spire, and is often toned with pink in the aperture.

Strombus (Tricornis) costatus

Strombus (Tricornis) galeatus

Strombus (Tricornis) gallus

Strombus (Tricornis) gigas

79

STROMBUS (TRICORNIS) GALLUS Linnaeus, 1758: Relatively thin, glossy. Body whorl with widely spaced spiral ridges dorsally; columella smooth except for traces of weak lirae posteriorly; outer lip very broadly flared, relatively thin, with a long, narrow, tubular posterior canal; traces of widely spaced spiral grooves at margin; notch distinct; anterior canal long, dorsally curved. Spire tall, with prominently projecting heavy knobs; shoulder with three or more very high, laterally flattened knobs in a single row. Cream dorsally, usually heavily spotted and blotched with brown or occasionally pinkish or lavender; columellar callus thick, tinged with salmon or pink; mouth white, tinged with salmon near margin. Carolinas south through Caribbean to Brazil; uncommon. Length 75-166mm. Other narrowly winged forms differ as follows: *oldi*—broader winged, brown mouth; *peruvianus*—different shape and color; *tricornis*—anterior canal shorter, dorsal knobs axially flattened.

STROMBUS (TRICORNIS) GIGAS Linnaeus, 1758: Very large, thick, rather glossy. Body whorl weakly spirally ridged dorsally; columella smooth except for weak lirae posteriorly; outer lip very broadly flared, thick or relatively thin, with a pointed posterior wing that equals or exceeds the spire; margin of lip weakly crenulate; notch distinct. Spire tall, sharply pointed, with heavy projecting pointed knobs on all whorls; very high pointed knobs on shoulder. Pale tan dorsally; columellar callus weakly developed, often tinged with deep pink; mouth deep pink within, white marginally. Carolinas south through Caribbean to Brazil; common. Length 150-290mm. The very large size of adults and very large pointed shoulder and spire knobs are distinct, especially when combined with the large expansion of the lip. Shells in specimen condition are difficult to find, although juveniles (rollers) and "souvenir" shells of the queen conch are abundant.

STROMBUS (TRICORNIS) GOLIATH Schroeter, 1805: Extremely large, very thick and heavy, rough. Body whorl with weak spiral ridges dorsally; columella smooth except for weak lirae posteriorly; outer lip very thick, broadly flared, with very high posterior wing or expansion that exceeds the spire; a greatly thickened ridge before the margin; notch obsolete in adults. Spire rather tall, sharply pointed, with low knobs; shoulder with many low or nearly obsolete knobs. Pale tan to cream dorsally, cream ventrally on the thick columellar callus; callus and mouth tinged with pink or orange, mouth whitish marginally. Restricted to central and southern Brazil; not uncommon, but currently very expensive. Length 275-375mm. The very high posterior lip expansion resembles *S. latissimus*, but at that point the similarity ends; *S. galeatus* is much more similar but has the lip lower posteriorly.

STROMBUS (TRICORNIS) LATISSIMUS Linnaeus, 1758: Moderate in size but extremely thick and heavy, moderately glossy. Body whorl with traces of a few raised nodulose spiral ridges and heavy axial threads; columella smooth; outer lip very thick, broadly flared, with a very high posterior expansion that exceeds the spire; a greatly thickened ridge before the margin; notch very deep and well defined. Spire moderate, with a few large rounded knobs; shoulder with faint traces of knobs and a single large knob at the left margin. Streaky tan or brown dorsally, ventrally with brighter reddish brown axial streaking enclosing triangular white spots; columellar callus very thick, often tinged with pink or salmon; mouth white within, weakly or strongly tinged with pink or salmon marginally. Western Pacific, southern Japan to Indonesia and Fiji; uncommon in most areas. Length 110-204mm. The lip is much higher than in most species of similar size, and the single large dorsal knob and strong notch are also distinctive.

Strombus (Tricornis) goliath

Strombus (Tricornis) latissimus

Strombus (Tricornis) oldi, live-taken; Dr. H. Lee photo

Strombus (Tricornis) oldi, beach shell

STROMBUS (TRICORNIS) OLDI Emerson, 1965: Relatively thin, glossy. Body whorl with 2-3 low nodulose spiral ridges and traces of others; columella smooth except for low lirae posteriorly; outer lip thin, crenulate at the margin, narrowly flared, with a high broad posterior wing equal to the spire; low broad ridges inside the aperture; notch shallow. Spire tall, the spiral ridges nearly obsolete, but the marginal knobs large; shoulder with 4 or more laterally flattened rounded knobs. Streaked with brown or tan on cream dorsally and ventrally; columellar callus thin, with a broad brown band; mouth creamy white, broadly stained brown within and posteriorly. Known from Somalia and perhaps Kenya on the East African coast, and recently discovered in the Muscat area, so presumably more widely distributed. At the moment this is the rarest species of *Strombus*. 95-150mm long. Similar to *S. gallus* and *S. tricornis,* but with a unique combination of brown in the mouth, a broader wing, and laterally flattened shoulder knobs. Also bears some similarity to *S. sinuatus* and *S. latus.*

STROMBUS (TRICORNIS) PERUVIANUS Swainson, 1823: Moderately thick, glossy. Body whorl with two weakly nodulose spiral ridges and several weaker rows; columella with several lirae posteriorly, some strong; outer lip thickened, narrowly flaring and nearly straight; posterior expansion higher than spire, distinctly triangular, with a deep ventral groove; notch deep. Spire low, broad, weakly nodulose; shoulder with several low knobs, the middle one very high. Rusty brown dorsally and ventrally with scattered white spots and blotches; columellar callus thick, orangish or salmon; mouth whitish deep within, otherwise distinctly salmon to orange. Eastern Pacific, Gulf of California to Ecuador; common. 60-198mm long. The triangular posterior lip expansion and bright colors distinguish it from *S. tricornis* and *S. gallus; S. raninus* is smaller, has heavier sculpture, and usually lacks the distinctive expansion.

STROMBUS (TRICORNIS) RANINUS Gmelin, 1791: Moderately thick, rather glossy, small for the subgenus. Body whorl covered with coarse spiral ridges, two of which are distinctly nodulose; columella with distinct lirae at both ends in adults; outer lip very thick, with many distinct lirae within; posterior expansion short, narrow, often notched; stromboid notch distinct. Spire rather tall, with very weak nodules and often strong varices; shoulder with many low or high knobs, usually the middle knob high. Brownish to reddish dorsally, spotted with white; usually a narrow middorsal band of black and white mottling, this band very distinct ventrally and barely covered by the callus, which is thick only anteriorly and whitish or salmon; outer lip marginally, then broadly, toned with rose or salmon, mouth whitish deep within. Carolinas south through the Caribbean to Brazil; common. 30-100mm long. Unique in the subgenus by its strong sculpture and usually notched lip expansion as well as distinct color pattern.

Strombus (Tricornis) peruvianus

Strombus (Tricornis) raninus

Strombus (Tricornis) sinuatus

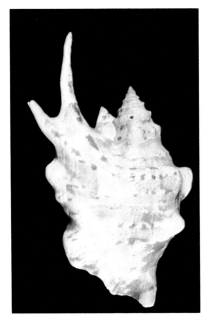 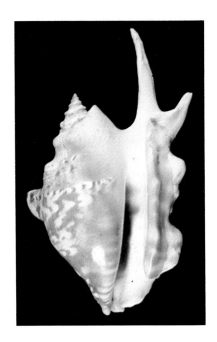

Strombus (Tricornis) taurus

87

STROMBUS (TRICORNIS) SINUATUS Humphrey, 1786: Rather thin, glossy. Body whorl covered with many fine spiral ridges, 2-3 of them heavier and weakly nodulose; columella smooth; outer lip thick, weakly crenulate at the margin, narrowly flared, with a broad posterior expansion equal to the spire and divided into 3-4 distinct flat digits; notch strongly defined; a strong sharp ridge inside the lip. Spire tall, pointed, with strong marginal knobs; shoulder with 3-4 distinct knobs, the middle one very high; traces of a low, long knob at the left margin. Cream mottled with tan to reddish brown dorsally, often with 2-3 narrow brown and white spiral bands; this mottled pattern continued ventrally, where brighter; columellar callus rather thin, pale salmon-brown, darker within; outer lip pinkish salmon or bright tan, becoming deep purplish brown within. Western Pacific, southern Japan to western Australia and Fiji; uncommon. 85-120mm long. The flat digits and bright mouth are unique.

STROMBUS (TRICORNIS) TAURUS Reeve, 1857: Thick and heavy, glossy if in good condition. Body whorl with 2-3 low spiral ridges that are nodulose and with traces of other ridges; columella smooth; outer lip very thick, with at least 2-3 lateral expansions plus a posterior expansion consisting of a flat, pointed callus under the spire, a very long and slender spine, and a shorter outer spine; a strong sharp ridge inside the margin; notch strongly developed. Spire tall, with heavy marginal knobs; shoulder with two strong knobs; an oblique heavy knob at middle of shell. White mottled with tan to rusty brown, usually eroded dorsally but bright ventrally; columellar callus thick and ridge-like, tan; mouth purple-brown deep within then white, margin with brown bands. Marshall and Marianas Islands, central Pacific; rare in good condition. 80-102mm long. Somewhat similar to *S. sinuatus,* but the very long slender posterior spine and the heavy oblique dorsal knob are unique.

STROMBUS (TRICORNIS) THERSITES Swainson, 1823: Extremely thick and heavy, dull. Body whorl with traces of spiral ridges dorsally, 2-3 weakly nodulose; columella smooth; outer lip very thick, with a rounded posterior expansion much shorter than spire; a strong ridge below the margin; notch strongly developed. Spire tall, very slender, with coarse knobs; shoulder with a large knob on the left side and 1-3 weaker ones. Cream above and below, irregularly mottled with brown (but usually eroded); columellar callus very thick, white to orange; mouth white, the margin with brown bars. Spottily distributed in the western Pacific, with records from the Ryukyus, Taiwan, New Guinea, Queensland, New Caledonia, Tonga, and French Polynesia; very uncommon. Length 100-170mm. Very much like *S. latissimus,* with a lower posterior expansion and very slender, tall spire.

STROMBUS (TRICORNIS) TRICORNIS Humphrey, 1786: Moderately thick, glossy; body whorl nearly smooth, with traces of spiral ridges; columella smooth, as is mouth; outer lip flared, thick at the margin, with a long narrow or triangular posterior canal that is closed in adults; notch well developed; anterior canal normal. Spire tall, with rounded marginal knobs; shoulder with about four axially flattened knobs, the middle one much the largest. Cream above and below, variably streaked and mottled with tan to dark brown; columellar callus whitish; mouth whitish to pale pinkish. Red Sea and Gulf of Aden; common. 64-125mm long. Somewhat intermediate in shape between *S. peruvianus* and *S. gallus,* but with heavier dorsal knobs, normal anterior canal, and duller colors.

Strombus (Tricornis) thersites

Strombus (Tricornis) tricornis

Strombus (Canarium) dentatus

Strombus (Canarium) erythrinus

91

STROMBUS (CANARIUM) DENTATUS Linnaeus, 1758: Elongated, round-shouldered. Spire whorls and posterior quarter of body whorl with numerous heavy axial folds. Aperture not reaching shoulder; columellar callus heavy, white, only the extreme anterior tip blackish internally and with faint teeth at both ends; outer lip much shorter than columella, anteriorly with 3-4 distinct flat teeth in adults; mouth heavily but finely lirate with white, appearing black in adults; notch shallow. Creamy white with orange or tan axial and spiral flammules, blotches, and spots; black of aperture visible externally on outer lip and projecting part of columella. Indo-Pacific (few records from Malaysia-Indonesia area) to Hawaii and French Polynesia; uncommon. 26-60mm long. The axial shoulder folds and white columella in combination are distinctive from the brown columella of *S. fragilis* and the smooth, white-mouthed *S. terebellatus*. Beware of juvenile *S. dentatus* (which lack teeth) being sold as other species.

STROMBUS (CANARIUM) ERYTHRINUS Dillwyn, 1817: Elongated, rather square-shouldered in appearance. Spire whorls and shoulder with numerous equal axial folds; trace of an enlarged knobby spiral ridge at midbody, plus fine spiral ridges anteriorly and on lip. Aperture not reaching shoulder; columellar callus heavy, lirate at least anteriorly and posteriorly, bicolored, blackish internally and white to dull orange externally; mouth mostly blackish in adults, finely lirate; notch strong. Cream to dull orange, usually with two broad darker bands on body whorl, the outer lip often blackish; very variable. Indo-Pacific, including Hawaii, east to the Gilbert Is. and New Caledonia; locally common. 20-50mm long. The shoulder knobs are finer than in *S. urceus* and shorter than in most *S. labiatus*. *S. rugosus* has a white mouth and columella, while *S. haemastoma* has the columella pink to violet.

STROMBUS (CANARIUM) FRAGILIS (Roeding, 1798): Elongated, round-shouldered. Entire shell smooth except for occasional presence of 1-2 indistinct axial folds on the shoulder and minute spiral threads that give a silky appearance to the shell. Aperture not reaching shoulder; columellar callus heavy, virtually smooth, solid brown; mouth solid brown, darkest near margin, very finely lirate; notch very shallow. White with irregular patches of tan and orange, the outer lip and anterior part of base brown. Western Pacific from Japan to Samoa and Hawaii; uncommon to rare in good condition. Length 24-50mm. More inflated than *S. terebellatus*, which lacks the heavy brown columellar callus; *S. dentatus* has teeth in adults, has many heavy folds on the shoulder, and lacks the dark brown on the columellar callus.

STROMBUS (CANARIUM) FUSIFORMIS Sowerby ii, 1842: Elongated, distinctly fusiform and very glossy, round-shouldered. Spire whorls with scattered varices, body whorl with two low rounded bumps or knobs on shoulder and some spiral ridges anteriorly. Aperture extending well above shoulder as a long posterior canal; columellar callus heavy, strongly lirate anteriorly and posteriorly, smooth or lirate at middle, white or tinged with pink to tan at ends and with a fine brown line marking the edge of the callus; mouth narrow, white within, orange to tan on edge, with heavy but short and regular lirae; notch distinct to weak. Whitish with orange or tan mottling and often 2-4 broad indistinct tan spiral bands; edge of lip often with distinct banding. Western Indian Ocean, Gulf of Aden and Red Sea to Mozambique, including some islands; locally common. 20-45mm long. The fusiform shape, weakly colored aperture, and long posterior canal are distinctive of this small conch.

Strombus (Canarium) fragilis

Strombus (Canarium) fusiformis

Strombus (Canarium) haemastoma

Strombus (Canarium) helli

STROMBUS (CANARIUM) HAEMASTOMA Sowerby ii, 1842: Elongate-oval (shape variable), round-shouldered. Spire whorls with heavy axial ridges and varices; shoulder with strong axial knobs and often a weaker second row below; entire body whorl often with heavy axial ridges (especially ventrally) and finer spiral ridges. Aperture usually not reaching shoulder; columellar callus moderate, with heavy lirae (teeth) at least anteriorly and posteriorly, bright pink to reddish tan or violet; mouth white within, lirate at the margin, with a heavy ridge external to the edge; usually a bright pink to reddish tan band across edge; notch distinct. Creamy to pale violet, with or without yellowish blotches, outer lip often reddish. Scattered in the Indo-Pacific; very uncommon to rare. 14-21mm long. *S. helli* is usually more oval with very strong columellar lirae and a dark violet mouth. *S. wilsoni* is smoother and has only an anterior black spot on the otherwise white and nearly smooth columella.

STROMBUS (CANARIUM) HELLI Kiener, 1843: Very similar to *S. haemastoma* and probably would be best considered a Hawaiian subspecies of that species. Differs in the more rotund body whorl and the shorter spire that is not equal to the body whorl (spire length variable in both species). The columellar callus is strongly lirate and deep violet in color, as is the edge of the mouth. Entire shell may be cream with brownish or yellow blotches or mostly bright tan with two broad white spiral bands; outer lip violet externally. Hawaiian chain only; uncommon. 14-27mm long. There is considerable variation in both shape and color pattern.

STROMBUS (CANARIUM) LABIATUS LABIATUS

(Roeding, 1798): Strongly shouldered. Spire whorls with numerous strong marginal knobs; shoulder with at least four knobs, one or two larger than the others; ventral surface usually with many heavy axial folds. Aperture thick at margin, not reaching shoulder; columellar callus thick, with numerous fine lirae over its entire length, orange or lavender-gray on white; mouth strongly white-lirate, with broad grayish to orangish band at the margin; notch well developed. Color extremely variable, white to solid dark brown, but usually tan or gray with spiral white bands. The typical subspecies has the columellar callus orange or yellowish with fine, slightly paler lirae, the margin of the mouth often orangish. Western Pacific, southern Japan to Fiji; also Andamans in the Indian Ocean. Length 16-47mm. *S. labiatus* is similar to *S. urceus* in shape and often pattern, but has a non-white, wholly lirate columellar callus and usually strong ventral folds; it also lacks the blackish blotch in the anterior canal usually found in *S. urceus*. *S. erythrinus* and *S. klineorum* have bicolored columellar calluses.

STROMBUS (CANARIUM) LABIATUS OLYDIUS

Duclos, 1844: Very similar to the typical subspecies in shape, sculpture, color pattern, and variability. However, the columellar callus is grayish to lavender with broad conspicuous white lirae, so it looks white with grayish streaks; the mouth is similarly colored. Indian Ocean, India to eastern Africa and Mauritius; uncommon. 20-48mm long. The typical subspecies has the columella orange, and *S. urceus* has columellar lirae only at the ends.

Strombus (Canarium) labiatus labiatus

Strombus (Canarium) labiatus olydius

Strombus (Canarium) klineorum

Strombus (Canarium) maculatus

STROMBUS (CANARIUM) KLINEORUM Abbott, 1960: Strongly shouldered. Spire whorls with numerous strong marginal knobs; shoulder with 3 knobs (the middle one very large) and some spiral ridges. Aperture thick, reaching shoulder; columellar callus thick, with strong teeth anteriorly and posteriorly but smooth over most of its length; callus distinctly bicolored, bright orange to red on outside, blackish inside; outer lip strongly lirate, mostly blackish, whitish deep within; notch well developed. Creamy white, heavily mottled with brown and grayish, usually with 2-4 narrow spiral white lines on dorsum; anterior half of dorsum commonly bright orange-tan; usually badly eroded and calcified. Known only from Sri Lanka; common but very hard to obtain. Length 17-37mm. Very much like *S. labiatus* or *S. urceus* in appearance but with fewer shoulder knobs and a strongly bicolored columellar callus. *S. microurceus* and *S. erythrinus* may have similar calluses, but both these species are lighter in weight, more round-shouldered, and have different shoulder knobs.

STROMBUS (CANARIUM) MACULATUS Sowerby ii, 1842: Rather oval, round-shouldered. Spire whorls with very fine tubercles and heavy varices; shoulder smooth or with 1-3 low knobs; fine spiral ridges over whole shell. Aperture thick, reaching shoulder or not, the mouth nearly square anteriorly and narrow posteriorly; columellar callus white, with strong lirae anteriorly and posteriorly but smooth at middle; mouth white, with strong marginal lirae; notch weak. White to pale yellow with 2-3 broad broken spiral brown bands, or blotched with brown; shoulder often with rather greenish square blotches; specimens from Easter Island and the Tuamotus are axially flammulated with chestnut (var. *depauperatus* Dautzenberg & Bouge). Islands of the central and western Pacific, Palau to Hawaii and south to Cook and Easter Is.; abundant to common. 8-36mm long. Very similar in shape and pattern to *S. mutabilis, S. microurceus,* and *S. wilsoni,* but differing from these species in the uniformly white columellar callus and mouth, the columella smooth at the middle.

STROMBUS (CANARIUM) MICROURCEUS (Kira, 1959): Rather oval, round-shouldered. Spire whorls with very fine tubercles and weak varices; shoulder smooth or with up to 6 low blunt knobs; fine spiral ridges on the outer lip. Aperture thick at margin, rather narrow, usually not reaching the shoulder; columellar callus thick, bicolored, yellow to orange outside and blackish inside with fine yellowish lirae that are weak at the middle of the callus; mouth white or pink within, broadly bordered by a blackish band with fine pale lirae; notch strong. Whitish or yellowish mottled and banded with tan or orange and with narrow white spiral bands; anterior canal long, with a large blackish blotch; sometimes a greenish blotch on the shoulder behind the lip. Western and central Pacific from southern Japan to Indonesia and east to Samoa; locally common, but hard to obtain. Length 14-30mm. In shape like a *S. mutabilis* or *S. maculatus*, but with a bicolored columellar callus and a long anterior canal with a dark blotch.

STROMBUS (CANARIUM) RUGOSUS Sowerby i, 1825: Extremely close to some forms of *S. erythrinus* and probably best considered a subspecies of that species regardless of supposed sympatry. Differs in the heavier and coarser spiral ridges on the body whorl, the stronger shoulder knobs, stronger knobs around midbody, and more shouldered appearance. More obviously, the mouth and columellar callus are white, not blackish, and the columellar callus has teeth only at the top and bottom. Southeastern Pacific, Fiji, Ellice Is., Samoa, and Tonga; uncommon, very hard to obtain. 20-50mm long.

Strombus (Canarium) microurceus

Strombus (Canarium) rugosus

Strombus (Canarium) mutabilis

Strombus (Canarium) mutabilis variety *ochroglottis*

STROMBUS (CANARIUM) MUTABILIS Swainson, 1821: Rather oval, round-shouldered. Spire whorls with fine tubercles and weak varices; shoulder with 3-4 (occasionally none) low knobs and fine spiral threads. Aperture thick marginally, reaching shoulder or not, the mouth narrow, especially posteriorly; columellar callus thick, with strong anterior and posterior teeth and weaker lirae that may be absent at the middle, pinkish to white with the lirae white; mouth deep pink or, rarely, chrome-yellow, strongly lirate; notch well defined. White to pale yellowish or orange, with 2-3 broad broken bands, small spots, fine spiral white lines, and usually dark brown to greenish blotches on the shoulder; very variable. Indo-Pacific, but not Hawaii, abundant. 15-40mm long. An apparently ecological variant (var. *ochroglottis* Abbott) with chrome-yellow aperture occurs in Mauritius and the Red Sea, with similar specimens in French Polynesia. Variety *zebriolatus* Adams & Leloup is axially streaked with brown; uncommon. Like *S. maculatus* in shape and sculpture, but usually lirate over the entire columellar callus (or nearly so) and with the mouth strongly colored.

STROMBUS (CANARIUM) TEREBELLATUS TERE-BELLATUS Sowerby ii, 1842: Elongated, fusiform, round-shouldered, and glossy. Spire and body whorl practically smooth. Aperture short, wide, not reaching shoulder in most specimens and not equalling anterior canal; columellar callus weak or absent, untoothed; aperture not lirate, whitish, sometimes with a few brown lines within; notch almost obsolete. Whitish to tan, variably spotted, blotched, and lineated with yellow, orange, or brown. The typical subspecies has the spire tall, usually ⅓ to ½ of the entire shell length, and sometimes has brown lines in the aperture. Western Pacific, southern Japan to Indonesia and Fiji; uncommon to rare. Length 28-46mm. *Strombus fragilis* and *S. dentatus* may be similar in form and color, but both have thicker columellar calluses and brown either on the callus or in the mouth, or both. *S. fusiformis* has a heavy callus and strong lirae.

STROMBUS (CANARIUM) TEREBELLATUS AFRO-BELLATUS Abbott, 1960: A very weakly distinguished subspecies with the spire shorter, ¼ to ⅓ the length of the shell, the brown apertural lines absent, and sometimes with a distinct posterior canal. Eastern Africa and Madagascar; uncommon or rare, very hard to obtain. Length 30-40mm. The recent discovery of apparently typical *S.t. terebellatus* in the Red Sea casts doubt on the validity of the eastern African subspecies, which is distinguished only by characters known to be variable in other *Strombus* species.

Strombus (Canarium) terebellatus terebellatus

Strombus (Canarium) terebellatus afrobellatus

Strombus (Canarium) urceus urceus

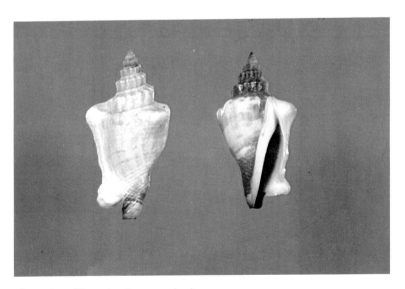

Strombus (Canarium) urceus incisus

STROMBUS (CANARIUM) URCEUS URCEUS Linnaeus, 1758: Thick, square-shouldered. Spire whorls with heavy axial folds, these continued onto the shoulder as small and large knobs, small ventrally, large dorsally (occasional shells smooth). Aperture reaching shoulder or not, thick, often square above, rather narrow; columellar callus thick, white toned with orange, with distinct lirations only at the ends, otherwise smooth; mouth heavily lirate, white to black within, usually orangish near the margin; a form with black mouth and columella (var. *ustulatus* Schumacher) is rather common; anterior canal with a black blotch; notch well developed to absent. Color highly variable, usually whitish or tan mottled and banded with darker. The typical subspecies has the spire sculpture and knobs moderately coarse, the aperture relatively broad and not reaching the shoulder, and the mouth and columella usually distinctly orange. Western Pacific, southern Japan to Indonesia and New Guinea; abundant. 18-61mm long. Very like *S. labiatus* and *S. klineorum*, but the columella not wholly lirate or bicolored. An extremely variable shell, the subspecies poorly distinguished; specimens approaching all three subspecies may be found in large Philippine lots.

STROMBUS (CANARIUM) URCEUS INCISUS Wood, 1828: Aperture and columellar callus greatly thickened posteriorly and forming a square margin that often projects beyond the shoulder. The lip below the notch is large and broad. Usually the pattern is reduced, the mouth brighter orange, and the anterior canal broadly marked with black. Restricted in typical form to the Solomons and New Hebrides, but similar specimens occur in New Guinea and (rarely) the Philippines; common. 20-60mm long.

STROMBUS (CANARIUM) URCEUS ORRAE Abbott, 1960: Knobs on the spire coarser than in the other subspecies, less numerous, with the shoulder knobs very large. The spire is typically very high; there may be strong axial folds on the ventral side of the body whorl as in *S. labiatus*. The orange of the mouth is subdued and may be absent. Northern and northwestern Australia; common. 20-50mm long.

STROMBUS (CANARIUM) WILSONI Abbott, 1967: Elongate-oval, glossy, rather round-shouldered. Spire with fine tubercles and varices; shoulder with numerous low axial folds or knobs; often many fine spiral ridges over entire shell. Aperture not quite reaching shoulder, narrow, with thick ridge behind the outer lip; columellar callus thick, smooth at center but weakly toothed at both ends; anterior teeth violet-brown, rest of columella whitish; mouth strongly lirate, with a violet-brown band darkest and widest anteriorly; notch strong. Color variable from uniformly cream or flesh with a few yellowish blotches to brown with white spots. Sporadic in the Indo-Pacific, Mozambique to Hawaii and Fiji; rare, hard to obtain. Length 18-30mm. This little shell differs from *S. microurceus* and *S. mutabilis* by its weakly toothed columella with a violet-brown spot at the base. *S. haemastoma* is very similar also and probably the closest relative, but it is more strongly sculptured and has broad reddish violet bands on the columella and mouth, as well as having the columella strongly lirate. *S. erythrinus* has a bicolored columella.

Strombus (Canarium) urceus orrae

Strombus (Canarium) wilsoni

110

Strombus (Dolomena) dilatatus

Strombus (Dolomena) labiosus

111

STROMBUS (DOLOMENA) DILATATUS Swainson, 1821: Moderately thick, the spire tall and heavily sculptured. Body whorl with many axial folds on the shoulder and spiral grooves anteriorly. Columellar callus thick, with weak teeth anteriorly and posteriorly, otherwise smooth, white; outer lip broadly flared, notched posteriorly and with a deep stromboid notch; posterior canal stopping at penult whorl or continuing in a broad curve across base of spire (var. *orosminus* Duclos); lirae heavy but not reaching edge of lip; purplish brown staining on lirae inside mouth. Cream or yellowish with several broad spiral bands of pale brown, or mottled. A supposed subspecies, *swainsoni* Reeve, of unknown distribution, is said to be distinguished by its larger size and heavier spiral ridges; it is not recognized here. Western Pacific, southern Japan to Indonesia and New Caledonia; also western Australia; common. 35-64mm long. *S. labiosus* has an upturned posterior lip; *S. plicatus* has heavy columellar teeth and staining; and *S. marginatus* is more darkly colored with a white mouth that is less flared, often with heavy dorsal tubercles or carinae.

STROMBUS (DOLOMENA) LABIOSUS Wood, 1828: Moderately heavy, with a strongly inflated body whorl. Spire tall and finely cancellate. Body whorl covered with distinct spiral ridges and four or more short axial folds that may be nearly obsolete or pointed. Columellar callus heavy anteriorly, indistinct posteriorly, with lirae that are strong at both ends but weak or absent in the middle, white; outer lip broadly flared, the posterior edge upturned; weak lirae in mouth often reach edge of lip at the shallow stromboid notch; mouth white, the lirae often stained purplish brown. Dorsum various shades of brown and gray, not distinctly banded, edge of lip white; white ventrally. Indo-Pacific, eastern Africa to Fiji; uncommon. Length 24-60mm. Somewhat similar to *S. dilatatus*, but the inflated body whorl and strongly but finely cancellate spire are distinctive, as are the upturned lip and grayish color. The spire sculpture reminds one of *Tibia (Rimella) crispata*.

STROMBUS (DOLOMENA) KLECKHAMAE Cernohorsky, 1971: Heavy, the spire moderate. Shoulder with 5-6 heavy axial knobs; spiral ridges fine. Columellar callus thick, with fine lirae posteriorly, then smooth, dark brown; outer lip broadly flared, the posterior canal short; lirae in aperture weak, indistinct; mouth usually dark brown, yellow deep within; notch deep. Dorsum tan or cream with dark spiral bands, the bands heaviest at suture (usually faded). Known from New Britain, Solomons, eastern Indonesia, and the Philippines; very rarely found living. 40-60mm long. Most specimens are subfossil. Readily distinguished by the form and dark brown mouth and columellar callus, although the mouth color may be variable; there is a broad dark band anteriorly on the body whorl that may be constant.

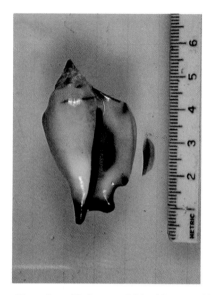

Strombus (Dolomena) kleckhamae, live-taken; Chapman photo

Strombus (Dolomena) kleckhamae, subfossil

Strombus (Dolomena) marginatus marginatus

Strombus (Dolomena) marginatus marginatus, weakly carinate
variety *robustus*

**STROMBUS (DOLOMENA) MARGINATUS MARGIN-
ATUS** Linnaeus, 1758: Moderately thick, the spire tall and
sculptured with low, closely spaced nodules and often weak
varices. Body whorl covered with fine spiral ridges, usually with a
distinct carina on the shoulder, this bearing one to several knobs.
Columellar callus thick, smooth except for weak lirae at both ends,
white; outer lip thick, moderately flared, deeply notched posteriorly with a long posterior canal that commonly extends onto the
spire; stromboid notch shallow; lirae in mouth heavy, commonly
reaching edge; mouth white. Dark or light brown, usually with
about 4-6 well defined spiral white bands, one on keel of body
whorl; pattern less distinct ventrally; whitish axial lines and flammules often present. The subspecies are poorly defined. The
typical subspecies (including *robustus* Sowerby as a synonym) is
distinguished by a distinct keel on the shoulder, this either smooth
or with several knobs; the shell is large, stout, the lip little flared.
Southern India to southern Japan; common. 29-75mm long. Very
similar to *S. dilatatus*, but the keel and knobs are distinctive.

**STROMBUS (DOLOMENA) MARGINATUS SEP-
TIMUS** Duclos, 1844: Very much flattened and with a strongly
flared lip compared to the other subspecies, the posterior canal not
extending onto the spire; the dorsum is darker brown with little
axial white pattern, but the spiral lines are strong. The knobs of
the spire whorls are usually stronger than in the other subspecies,
but there is seldom more than a trace of a single knob on the
shoulder, the carina very weak or absent. Western Pacific islands
from Okinawa and the Philippines south to New Caledonia; in-
tergrades with *S. m. marginatus* in Borneo and varying clinally
toward that subspecies north of the Philippines; uncommon.
25-65mm long.

**STROMBUS (DOLOMENA) MARGINATUS SUCCINC-
TUS** Linnaeus, 1767: Relatively more slender, with a distinctly
rounded shoulder bearing a single knob, the keel weak or absent;
color and pattern like typical *marginatus*, the lip thick and not
greatly flared. Spire sculpture relatively weak. Southeastern India
and Sri Lanka, in muddy water; sympatric with typical
marginatus, which usually occurs in coral areas; common.
40-55mm. Further work is necessary on this taxon, which can
technically be either a full species or just an ecological variant, but
not a true subspecies.

Strombus (Dolomena) marginatus septimus

Strombus (Dolomena) marginatus succinctus

118

Strombus (Dolomena) minimus

Strombus (Dolomena) plicatus plicatus, slightly subadult

STROMBUS (DOLOMENA) MINIMUS Linnaeus, 1771: Very small, thick, the spire with rounded closely spaced knobs and a few varices. Body whorl smooth except for 2-3 rounded knobs. Columellar callus extremely thick, extending posteriorly well onto spire, smooth except for a few weak teeth anteriorly; outer lip broadly flared, deeply notched posteriorly, and with a strong stromboid notch; margin of lip very thick, with weak lirae anteriorly; posterior canal broad, erect, almost equalling spire; mouth and columella strongly toned with bright yellow. Brown above with one or two indistinct spiral white bands or rows of spots; whitish ventrally, often with a thick callus covering the entire surface. Western Pacific, Ryukyus to Indonesia and Samoa; common. 14-30mm long, rarely to 40mm. The large upright posterior canal and matching extension of the columellar callus are distinctive.

STROMBUS (DOLOMENA) PLICATUS PLICATUS (Roeding, 1798): Moderately heavy, with a tall spire having numerous axial folds and a few varices. Body whorl with few to many axial folds, some developed into knobs on the shoulder; heavy spiral ridges often present. Columellar callus thick, with numerous lirae over most of its length, at least on the margin, often stained brown; outer lip broadly flared, shallowly notched posteriorly, the posterior canal usually short; strong lirae in mouth; mouth white to brown; stromboid notch weak to strong. Whitish, with indistinct broad pale or dark brown bands dorsally, seldom strongly patterned. In the typical subspecies the body whorl is inflated and covered ventrally with strong axial folds, the folds weaker dorsally but often visible; anterior canal short; columella with some light brown staining, but the mouth white. Red Sea, perhaps extending into northern Indian Ocean; rare. 45-62mm long. *S. plicatus* is very like *S. dilatatus* in shape and dorsal pattern but has a strongly lirate columellar callus and often brown staining in the mouth.

STROMBUS (DOLOMENA) PLICATUS COLUMBA

Lamarck, 1822: Like the typical subspecies in form, but with a longer anterior canal; the folds are absent ventrally on the body whorl and are very weak or absent dorsally, the knobs well developed. The columellar callus is variously blotched with brown, and in adults there are small or large brown areas in the mouth. Southeastern Africa, Madagascar, and to the Seychelles, perhaps with influence extending into the northern Indian Ocean; common. 33-47mm long.

STROMBUS (DOLOMENA) PLICATUS PULCHELLUS

Reeve, 1851: A small subspecies seldom exceeding 30mm; columellar callus and mouth largely brownish, often very dark; the dorsal surface is often mostly dark brown as well. The spire lacks distinct spiral ridges (present in *S. p. columba*). Western Pacific, southern Japan to Borneo and to Fiji; uncommon. 20-39mm long.

Strombus (Dolomena) plicatus columba

Strombus (Dolomena) plicatus pulchellus

Strombus (Dolomena) plicatus sibbaldi

Strombus (Dolomena) variabilis

STROMBUS (DOLOMENA) PLICATUS SIBBALDI
Sowerby ii, 1842: Sometimes considered a variant of *S.p. plicatus,*
but seems distinct. Much more broad-bodied, with the spire very
tall and slender. Axial folds absent or very weakly developed ventrally; the anterior canal is short. Columellar callus brown along
margin in adults, the mouth white. Northern Indian Ocean; uncommon. 30-40mm long. The very broad form with a slender
spire is distinctive. This was once considered a very rare
subspecies.

STROMBUS (DOLOMENA) VARIABILIS Swainson,
1820: Rather thin, glossy, the spire tall and with heavy axial folds
and varices. Body whorl smooth and shiny, with 2-4 heavy, rather
pointed nodules on the shoulder and a heavy fold at the left
margin. Columellar callus heavy anteriorly, smooth except for
weak anterior teeth, white except for a rather squarish tan or
yellowish blotch at middle (often absent); outer lip flared, very
thick at edge, shallowly notched posteriorly, the posterior canal
usually short; lirae absent or very weak; stromboid notch strong;
mouth glossy white. Dorsally white or pale yellowish with many
short axial tan blotches and lines, usually with several poorly
defined dark and light spiral bands; white ventrally with weaker
pattern. Western Pacific, Sumatra to Ryukyus and to Samoa; common. 25-60mm long. The color form *athenius* Duclos, usually
found near the southeastern edge of the range, is smaller and has
stronger color banding. Distinguished from *S. dilatatus* by the
lack of strong lirae in the mouth and any trace of color there, as
well as by the strong lateral fold.

STROMBUS (LABIOSTROMBUS) EPIDROMUS Linnaeus, 1758: Relatively light in weight, glossy, with a tall spire and a rounded shoulder. Body whorl with 2-5 low knobs or axial folds on the shoulder and traces of folds ventrally. Columellar callus thick, white, glossy, smooth; outer lip flaring, evenly rounded, very thick, the stromboid notch distinct; posterior canal rather short; no lirae in mouth, which is white. Pale yellowish to tan, with fine darker brown lines forming 2-3 very broad spiral bands; pattern often indistinct. Western Pacific, Ryukyus to Singapore and to New Caledonia; generally uncommon. Length 50-90mm. This is very much like *S. variabilis* in form but with a much more evenly rounded lip and no lirae.

STROMBUS (DOXANDER) CAMPBELLI Griffith & Pidgeon, 1834: Elongate, the spire with nearly flat sides; heavy axial folds on spire whorls, with a wide spiral ridge posteriorly on each whorl; body whorl with a heavy knob dorsally on the shoulder and usually a large axial fold on the left side. Columellar callus thick anteriorly, often weak posteriorly; outer lip flared, thick at edge, the posterior canal indistinct in most specimens; lirae of mouth weak; stromboid notch weak. Whitish to pale tan with broad darker tan spiral bands of fine axial lines; columella and mouth white. Northern Australia from Western Australia to New South Wales; common. 32-70mm long. Often considered a subspecies of *S. vittatus,* but the spire whorls are flat-sided and differently sculptured, the dorsal knob and lateral fold are usually very strong, and the posterior canal is weak.

Strombus (Labiostrombus) epidromus

Strombus (Doxander) campbelli

126

Strombus (Doxander) vittatus vittatus

Strombus (Doxander) vittatus japonicus

STROMBUS (DOXANDER) VITTATUS VITTATUS
Linnaeus, 1758: Elongated, the spire with rounded or shouldered whorls bearing heavy axial and spiral ridges, the axial folds often extending onto the body whorl; knob on shoulder weak. Columellar callus thick, white; outer lip strongly to weakly flared, moderately thick, the posterior canal well developed; lirae well developed in mouth; stromboid notch weak to strong. Pale to dark brown, usually with one or more spiral broken white bands. In the typical subspecies the spire whorls are rounded; the dorsum of the body whorl has only weak axial folds, a single knob, or no raised sculpture; the spiral ridging is restricted to the anterior third of the body whorl. Two forms of the typical subspecies occur, one with a rather low spire, weak body sculpture, and relatively flared mouth, the other (var. *australis* Schroeter) with an extremely tall spire, larger size, heavy folds on the body whorl, and relatively narrower mouth. Western Pacific, Ryukyus to Indonesia and to the Fiji Islands; moderately common. 35-100mm long. Very like *S. campbelli,* but the spire whorls different and the body without two heavy knobs.

STROMBUS (DOXANDER) VITTATUS JAPONICUS
Reeve, 1851: Wider, darker brown, with a stronger white pattern. This is a more heavily sculptured subspecies, the spire with more angled margins and stronger ridges, the body whorl with distinct axial folds dorsally often forming several knobs, and strong spiral ribs over most of the body whorl. Apparently restricted to southern Japan; moderately common. 45-70mm long. At first glance more similar to a gigantic *S. marginatus septimus* and quite distinct from typical *vittatus.*

STROMBUS (DOXANDER) LISTERI Gray, 1852: Very large and elegant, elongate, glossy; early whorls with strong axial and spiral ridges, the sides rounded; later whorls and body whorl nearly smooth. Columellar callus rather thin, often incomplete posteriorly; outer lip very broad, greatly flared, with a large, erect upswept wing posteriorly and a deep, wide stromboid notch; posterior canal very short; mouth lirae absent, but a strong ridge is present within the mouth. Pale to dark brown with 2-5 or more spiral bands of brown and white blotches; later spire whorls with strong axial brown flammules; columella and mouth white, often with a strong violet tinge. Northern Indian Ocean, Gulf of Oman to Thailand; uncommon. Length 90-160mm. Although recently placed in the subgenus *Euprotomus* on anatomical grounds, the shell definitely indicates a close resemblance to *S. vittatus,* from which it differs in the wing, lack of mouth lirae, and the more distinct color pattern, as well as the much greater size.

STROMBUS (LENTIGO) FASCIATUS Born, 1778: Small, thin, light; body whorl smooth except for heavy triangular spines on the shoulder, these sometimes weak or even absent. Columellar callus thin, indistinct, smooth, usually yellowish; outer lip thin, the stromboid notch weak; mouth smooth, yellowish, sometimes pale orange or pale pink. Body whorl white with pink or tan tones, with about 5-8 narrow, sometimes broken, blackish or brownish spiral lines. Restricted to the Red Sea; common. Length 30-50mm (usually less than 40mm). Unique in combining black lines, a yellowish mouth, and strong shoulder spines. The spines make the shell look like a miniature juvenile *S. gigas.* This species bears little obvious resemblance to the other species of *Lentigo.*

Strombus (Doxander) listeri

Strombus (Lentigo) fasciatus

Strombus (Lentigo) granulatus

Strombus (Lentigo) latus

STROMBUS (LENTIGO) GRANULATUS Swainson, 1822: Thick, heavy, dull; spire tall, slender, the knobs heavy; body whorl with very heavy shoulder knobs and 3-4 weaker knob rows. Columellar callus thick, often stained cream; outer lip thick only in full adults, straight at the margin, with traces of weak irregular lirae; mouth white; stromboid notch moderate; posterior canal poorly developed. Whitish, with traces of brown bands, stronger ventrally; juveniles often reddish, violet, or pinkish. Gulf of California to Ecuador; common (full adults hard to obtain). 40-80mm long. Narrower and with a taller spire than *S. latus*, the appearance much rougher and more nodulose at similar sizes. *S. lentiginosus* and *S. pipus* have colored apertures, shorter spires, and complicated posterior canals.

STROMBUS (LENTIGO) LATUS Gmelin, 1791: Thick, heavy, often glossy; spire relatively short and wide, the knobs smaller than in most other species; body whorl of full adults with very heavy triangular shoulder spines and 2-4 rows of weaker knobs, these often absent in large subadults and some adults. Columellar callus often thin posteriorly, smooth, whitish; outer lip thick, wavy, rather flared, with short, weak lirae in full adults; mouth whitish; stromboid notch moderate; posterior canal rounded, weakly developed. Medium brown with scattered white spots or blotches; pinkish bands at shoulder, midbody, and often spire whorls sometimes strong. Western Africa from the Cape Verde Is. to Angola plus the mid-Atlantic islands; moderately common, full adults hard to obtain. 75-160mm long. Broader and lower-spired than *S. granulatus*, this species often looks amazingly like *S. (Strombus) alatus*.

STROMBUS (LENTIGO) LENTIGINOSUS Linnaeus, 1758: Thick, heavy, dull; spire moderately high, with heavy knobs; body whorl with very large knobs on the shoulder and three or more rows of lower knobs. Columellar callus thick anteriorly, white but often with a silver glaze; the entire ventral surface is glossy; a callus on lower spire whorls; outer lip thick, crenulate, rather straight, without lirae; mouth deep orange or salmon within, becoming creamy externally; posterior canal deep, usually with two distinct lobes above the notch; stromboid notch deep, the lip anterior to it crenulate. Creamy or silvery white with irregular brown blotches in vaguely spiral bands. Indo-Pacific, eastern Africa to French Polynesia, not recorded from the Red Sea area or Hawaii; common. Length 55-104mm. The lobed posterior canal, orange mouth, and lack of lirae are distinctive.

STROMBUS (LENTIGO) PIPUS (Roeding, 1798): Moderately thick, dull; spire rather high, with heavy knobs; shoulder of full adults usually with heavy knobs, plus 3-5 rows of smaller, often rather pointed, knobs on rest of body whorl. Columellar callus rather thin, especially posteriorly, white or cream; entire ventral surface often glossy, callused; outer lip moderately flared, the margin crenulate; posterior canal strong above a deep notch, often crenulate; mouth with many strong lirae in adults, deep purplish brown (smooth and white in juveniles); stromboid notch deep, the anterior lobe crenulate. White with irregular tan mottling dorsally and ventrally. Indo-Pacific, eastern Africa to French Polynesia, not known from the northern Indian Ocean and the island groups of the central Pacific; somewhat uncommon, especially full adults. Length 38-70mm. The dark, lirate mouth will distinguish *S. pipus* from all species when adult.

Strombus (Lentigo) lentiginosus

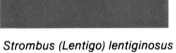

Strombus (Lentigo) pipus

134

Strombus (Euprotomus) aratrum

Strombus (Euprotomus) aurisdianae

STROMBUS (EUPROTOMUS) ARATRUM (Roeding, 1798): Spire with heavy, rather sharp knobs on the whorls; shoulder with a row of about 5-7 very large, pointed knobs; whole body whorl covered with heavy spiral ridges, two ridges with strong but low knobs. Columellar callus anteriorly very thick, whitish to tan, posteriorly only a glaze that barely hides the sculpture; a small blackish callus (occasionally yellow) at top of body whorl and last spire whorl; mouth with weak lirae posteriorly, otherwise smooth; posterior projection (wing) rather wide, usually black; mouth pale creamy orange to deep orange. Rusty dull brown above with some darker lines and blotches, usually with black bands and areas along outer lip. Spottily distributed in western Pacific and also found in Bay of Bengal; uncommon. 55-100mm long. Very much like *S. aurisdianae* in form except for the somewhat more elongated spire with heavier knobs and the wider aperture; when present, the black callus and mouth margining are very distinctive. Variety *chrysostomus* Kuroda is a form in which the black callus is absent.

STROMBUS (EUPROTOMUS) AURISDIANAE Linnaeus, 1758: Spire with weak or well developed knobs; shoulder with a row of 5-7 moderate to large knobs; whole body whorl covered with strong spiral ridges, 2-3 ridges with low knobs; columellar callus thick, white or pale cream, often continued onto spire; mouth relatively narrow, with weak lirae posteriorly; sometimes lirae present at extreme anterior end; posterior projection (wing) often short, whitish; mouth deep orange or salmon within, broadly bordered with white or cream. Grayish to dull brown above, not very shiny, with scattered darker brown spots or lines; mouth with pale brown lines on margins. Indo-West Pacific, eastern Africa to the Solomons; common, but seemingly not recorded from the northwestern Indian Ocean. Length 46-80mm. The absence of strong and numerous lirae distinguishes *S. aurisdianae* from *S. vomer*, while the rough and dull surface distinguishes it from *S. bulla*. *S. aratrum* is usually more elongated with a wider aperture and is heavily marked with blackish, the mouth usually not bordered with white.

STROMBUS (EUPROTOMUS) BULLA (Roeding, 1798):
Spire with rather heavy knobs; shoulder with about 5-7 heavy
knobs, the body whorl otherwise smooth and glossy above and
below. Columellar callus thick anteriorly, continued onto spire to
tip, white, usually covering sculpture; mouth rather narrow,
smooth within, and without obvious lirae; wing often very long
and slender; mouth deep bright orange, usually bordered by
white. Dorsum bright pinkish brown or dark brown, with
numerous small white dots fused into larger blotches and lines.
Western Pacific, Ryukyus to Indonesia and Samoa; common.
49-72mm long. The presence of only one row of dorsal knobs on a
polished and brightly colored surface is distinctive when combined with an absence of apertural lirae.

STROMBUS (EUPROTOMUS) VOMER VOMER (Roed-
ing, 1798): Thick and heavy, relatively elongated and narrow; in
dorsal view the row of large shoulder knobs is at about midlength
of the shell (well posterior to midbody in related species); spire
knobs very large; shoulder knobs usually large and pointed, rest of
body whorl with strong spiral ridges, 2-3 of these often nodulose.
Columellar callus very thick anteriorly, posteriorly very thin,
barely covering sculpture; another smaller callus on lower spire
whorls; calluses white or creamy tan; mouth strongly lirate
throughout; wing long and rather narrow. In the typical
subspecies the mouth is orange with white lirae, there is a large
brown stain on the posterior part of the columella, and the dorsum
is relatively glossy pinkish brown with white dots. Sporadic in the
western Pacific, recorded from the Ryukyus, New Caledonia, and
Tonga, possibly also New Guinea and Queensland; uncommon to
rare. Length 55-100mm. The many strong apertural lirae
distinguish this species, while the smooth finish and orange mouth
distinguish the subspecies.

Strombus (Euprotomus) bulla

Strombus (Euprotomus) vomer vomer

Strombus (Euprotomus) vomer hawaiensis, subadult

Strombus (Euprotomus) vomer iredalei

STROMBUS (EUPROTOMUS) VOMER HAWAIENSIS
Pilsbry, 1917: Similar in shape to the nominate subspecies, but
differing in having the mouth white or cream and the dorsum with
strong spiral ridges of about equal size, so dull and rough in appearance. Restricted to the Hawaiian chain; rare. 64-106mm long.

STROMBUS (EUPROTOMUS) VOMER IREDALEI Ab-
bott, 1960: Virtually identical to *S. v. hawaiensis* in shape, dull appearance, and pale mouth. Differs mainly in having two spiral
ridges on the dorsum below the shoulder area enlarged and often
nodulose, not all even-sized as in *hawaiensis*. Western and northern Australia; common. 37-100mm long. It is probably impossible
to distinguish individual specimens of *hawaiensis* and *iredalei* in all
cases, which should be remembered when purchasing *hawaiensis*
at 20-30 times the price of *iredalei*.

STROMBUS (CONOMUREX) DECORUS DECORUS

(Roeding, 1798): Conical, low-spired, thick and heavy; spire whorls with axial folds that may be absent or reduced, the shoulder usually with weak folds; rest of shell smooth, glossy. Columella without a distinct callus; mouth rather narrow, not flared, with a deep posterior notch and deep or moderate stromboid notch. White with brown spots and blotches or reticulations in spiral rows; columella white or spotted with brown; mouth pale orange within, broadly margined with white, including the posterior canal. The nominate subspecies is narrower than the next and less conical, with a darker aperture. Indian Ocean; moderately common. Length 34-75mm. In *S. luhuanus* the columella is black.

STROMBUS (CONOMUREX) DECORUS PERSICUS

Swainson, 1821: Barely distinguishable from the typical subspecies by the more strongly conical, broader form, more flared mouth that is very pale orange within, and nearly obsolete spire and shoulder folds. Restricted to the Arabian area; uncommon. Length 40-51mm.

Strombus (Conomurex) decorus decorus

Strombus (Conomurex) decorus persicus

142

Strombus (Conomurex) luhuanus

Strombus (Gibberulus) gibberulus gibberulus

STROMBUS (CONOMUREX) LUHUANUS Linnaeus, 1758: Conical, thick, rather glossy, with a low spire; spire whorls smooth or with axial folds; body whorl smooth except shoulder may be weakly plicate. Columellar callus narrow, thin, black exteriorly and rosy or orange within; mouth narrow, not flared, the posterior and stromboid notches deep. White with pale brown blotches arranged in narrow and broad spiral bands, often entirely white or entirely brown, mouth completely deep rose or salmon-orange, including margin and posterior canal. Western Pacific, from Japan to Queensland and east to Fiji and Line Islands; common. Length 32-80mm. The conical shape is shared only with *S. decorus,* but the uniformly colored mouth and black columella are very distinctive.

STROMBUS (GIBBERULUS) GIBBERULUS GIBBER-ULUS Linnaeus, 1758: Moderately thick, the spire rather low, with many heavy varices and apparent breaks; spire and body whorl appear distorted, in lateral view the posterior part of the body whorl projecting ventrally beyond the last spire whorl. Outer lip not greatly thickened, with strong posterior and stromboid notches, weakly lirate within; columellar callus rather thin, white. In the typical subspecies the color is very uniform, whitish with many closely spaced narrow brown lines dorsally and ventrally; columella white, often with a purple blotch well within; mouth strongly tinted with purple. Indian Ocean; common but now hard to obtain. 30-70mm long. The distorted shape is approached only by *S. fragilis,* which lacks the very heavy varices and differs in having a brown mouth and columella. The typical subspecies is more constant in color than *S. g. gibbosus,* with the columellar blotch, when present, not easily visible in ventral view.

**STROMBUS (GIBBERULUS) GIBBERULUS GIB-
BOSUS** (Roeding, 1798): Extremely variable in pattern and degree of distortion; usually variably mottled or lined with yellow to dark brown on white, seldom with the lines fine and uniform; aperture usually purple, often white, occasionally rosy; columellar blotch when present purple, easily visible in ventral view because it is on the face of the callus. Western Pacific to French Polynesia, not Hawaii; abundant. 30-70mm long. Recognized by its variability.

STROMBUS (GIBBERULUS) GIBBERULUS ALBUS
Moerch, 1850: More distorted than in the typical subspecies or *gibbosus;* pinkish white externally with a broad violet band above the suture; mouth deep rose. Restricted to the Red Sea and vicinity; common. 34-56mm long. The combination of pale uniform pinkish white color, violet band, and rose mouth is not found in the other subspecies, although each feature can occur individually in any population.

Strombus (Gibberulus) gibberulus gibbosus

Strombus (Gibberulus) gibberulus albus

Austroharpa exquisita exquisita

Austroharpa punctata punctata; P. Clover photo

AUSTROHARPA EXQUISITA (Iredale, 1931): Small, heavily sculptured with spiral and axial ridges. The protoconch is large and domed but with fewer than 3 full whorls. Length 22-46mm. Rare in deep water. Two weakly defined subspecies are recognizable. *A. e. exquisita* (Iredale), found in eastern Australia from southern Queensland to northern Tasmania and South Australia, is smaller (under 30mm), has the protoconch pale pinkish yellow, has the body whorl relatively wider and less distinctly shouldered, and has the spiral sculpture sometimes weak and irregular. In *A. e. loisae* Rehder, from southern Western Australia, the protoconch is darker yellow, the spiral sculpture is somewhat heavier and more regular, and the body whorl is a bit narrower and more strongly shouldered; adults are about 28-46mm long. Both subspecies are tan to grayish or yellowish with scattered small reddish brown specks and sometimes larger irregular blotches in two or three indistinct spiral rows.

AUSTROHARPA PUNCTATA (Verco, 1896): Small, glossy, with only axial ridges distinct on the body whorl (almost rib-like), although microscopic spiral sculpture may be visible. Protoconch large, domed, with fewer than 3 full whorls. Length 20-37mm. Rare in deep water. Two subspecies are recognizable. *A. p. punctata* (Verco), of South Australia, is very glossy, yellowish, with weak and widely spaced axial ridges, only 5-8 ridges visible on the body whorl in dorsal view; usually covered with small reddish brown spots and with larger blotches in about three spiral rows, but sometimes without pattern. Larger, 32-37mm long. *A. p. wilsoni* Rehder, from southern Western Australia, is a bit slenderer and more shouldered, with more axial ridges (7-12 in dorsal view); it is less glossy, white to pale yellowish with little spotting, and smaller, 20-26mm long.

HARPA AMOURETTA Roeding, 1798: Group A. Small or moderate in size, with very thin and very thick (variety *minor* Lamarck) variants. The ribs end in strong spines posteriorly and are marked with clusters of two to many narrow blackish lines. The umbilicus is indistinct. The ventral callus is often thick and usually has three rather squarish or rounded blotches that are well separated; either the posterior or columellar blotch, or both, may be absent. Adults 20-60mm long, variable from population to population. Common in the Indo-Pacific from eastern Africa and the Red Sea to Hawaii and French Polynesia. Very much like *H. gracilis*, but that species lacks rib spines and has white protoconch whorls (reddish in all other *Harpa*). *H. harpa* is broader and larger, usually has the outer lip finely toothed, and has a different pattern.

HARPA GRACILIS Broderip and Sowerby i, 1829: Group A. Small, thin, slender, with a white, not pinkish or reddish, protoconch. The ribs are slender, truncate posteriorly and without spines; they are marked with numerous clusters of narrow blackish lines. There is a narrow umbilicus behind the columella. Ventrally the blotches are poorly developed or absent and the columellar callus is absent or very poorly defined. Length 20-35mm. Rare in the southeastern Pacific, known from isolated localities in the Ellice and Line Islands as well as Clipperton Island off the Central American coast, but almost all specimens available to collectors come from the Tuamotus in French Polynesia. Similar to *H. amouretta* in general apperance, but readily distinguished by the lack of spines on the ribs and the white protoconch.

Harpa amouretta

Harpa gracilis

Harpa harpa

Harpa amouretta, live; Scott Johnson photo

151

HARPA HARPA (Linnaeus, 1758): Group A. Small to moderate in size, rather thick, usually widened below the shoulder. The ribs are rather wide and end in strong spines; they are marked with clusters of two to many narrow dark lines. The ventral blotches are usually distinct, but the columellar and posterior blotches may be small or absent in occasional specimens. In most specimens there are some dark brown to reddish spots on top of the shoulder and often large red squares at the broad part of the body whorl. The anterior margin of the outer lip is commonly finely spined or toothed. Adults usually 40-75mm. Widespread in the Indo-Pacific; rare in the Indian Ocean but common in the Pacific east to the Marshall Islands and French Polynesia. Specimens from the central Pacific may be small, very broad, and pale. *H. kajiyamai* Rehder is here considered an uncommon variant of *H. harpa* with the posterior blotch reduced or absent and the body whorl a bit narrower than usual. *H. harpa* is much like *H. amouretta* but is broader, has dark areas on the shoulder, and commonly has red squares; the lip in *H. amouretta* apparently is not toothed.

KAJIYAMAI

Ventral pattern of *Harpa harpa* var. *kajiyamai.*

HARPA CRENATA Swainson, 1822: Group B. A moderately large, rather thick species with relatively wide ribs and a rather dull finish. The ribs are strongly spined posteriorly, usually with 2-3 smaller but strong spines near the shoulder. The body whorl is broad and typically widened below the shoulder. The ribs are variably blotched but are paralleled by strong narrow axial brown dashes; if larger blotches are present between the ribs, they are chestnut or tan, not reddish. The columellar and midbody blotches are usually strong and widely separated, but the posterior blotch may be small or absent. 40-95mm long. Common in the Panamic area from Baja California to Colombia, apparently not on the offshore islands. Very close to *H. doris,* but usually wider and with stronger secondary rib spines; the large blotches in *H. doris* are usually reddish.

HARPA DORIS Roeding, 1798: Group B. Usually rather small, moderately to distinctly thick in texture, with a good gloss. The ribs are strongly spined posteriorly, sometimes with 2-3 smaller spines near the shoulder. Rather slender, the sides gently rounded. Ribs variably blotched with brown, but sharing with *H. crenata* the presence of distinct axial brown dashes at the sides of the ribs. Columellar and midbody blotches usually small but strong, the posterior blotch smaller and sometimes absent. Usually one or two spiral rows of pinkish to reddish blotches above midbody between the ribs. Length usually 30-80mm. Uncommon from the Bulge of western Africa to Angola, including Ascension I. and the Cape Verde Is. Very much like *H. crenata,* but more slender, with distinct reddish blotches and often weaker secondary rib spines.

Harpa crenata

Harpa doris

Harpa articularis

Harpa costata

155

HARPA ARTICULARIS Lamarck, 1822: Group C. Large, usually thin in texture, with many relatively slender axial ribs. In ventral view most of the surface of the body whorl is covered with smoky brown that only partially obscures the ribs and is not divided posteriorly; typically the columella is only narrowly marked with brown. The ribs usually have many wide and narrow dark lines in various patterns, seldom with broad orangish or pinkish bands. Length 40-100mm. Common from the Fiji area west to the Philippines and Okinawa, northern Australia, Indonesia, both shores of Malaysia, and Thailand. Likely to be confused only with some patterns of *H. davidis* (especially var. *major*), which is usually thicker, has the ventral blotch partially or entirely divided, and usually has the columella broadly marked with brown.

HARPA COSTATA (Linnaeus, 1758): Group C. Large, moderately thick, rather distinctly broader than most other harps, with the ribs narrower and numerous, usually over 30 on the body whorl. Whitish or yellowish with two or more narrow spiral bands of yellow, flesh, or orange over the body whorl and sometimes with indistinct flesh or chestnut spots. The mouth is often distinctly yellowish. The ventral blotches are usually large and dark but the posterior and midbody blotches may be connected at the mouth and the columellar blotch may be indistinct or absent. Adults 40-100mm long. Rare; the most expensive *Harpa*. Restricted to Mauritius and Rodrigues Is. in the southern Indian Ocean, but also reported from Madagascar. This species is very close to some *H. davidis* but distinct in the broader shape, more numerous ribs, and pale coloration.

HARPA DAVIDIS Roeding, 1798: Group C. Large, often thick, with relatively few wide to narrow axial ribs. In ventral view there are two or three blackish or dark brown blotches, usually with the posterior and midbody blotches fused near the mouth and divided by a narrow to wide yellowish to whitish triangle or band; the columellar blotch is very small to large and connected to the midbody blotch; occasionally all blotches are fused. The ribs have scattered narrow and wide lines variable in color from black to pink, the pink color sometimes present as broad bands. Adults 45-110mm. Widespread over the Indo-Pacific from eastern Africa to Hawaii and French Polynesia. The usually thicker texture and divided blotches will distinguish this species from *H. articularis*.

Three intergrading variants may be recognized. The typical variety, seemingly restricted to the northern Indian Ocean, often has rather narrow ribs and a small columellar blotch that is commonly widely separated from the midbody blotch. *H. davidis* var. *major* Roeding is the most commonly seen form; it occurs over the entire range of the species and is sympatric with the other two varieties. As a rule it is recognizable by the pale triangle dividing the posterior and midbody blotches being whitish and very distinct, with the columellar blotch large, dark, and widely fused with the midbody blotch, leaving the ventral surface largely dark. *H. davidis* var. *ventricosa* Lamarck is found only in the southern Indian Ocean and eastern Africa; it is often larger and thicker than the other variants, has wider ribs on the average, is marked with broad pale bands, and has the ventral blotches distinct and separated by broad pale areas, especially the posterior and midbody blotches. It is not uncommon to find all three variations and intermediates in a single Indian Ocean population.

Ventral patterns of *Harpa davidis* var. *ventricosa* and var. *major*.

VENTRICOSA   MAJOR

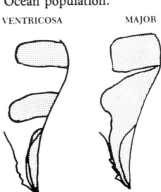

Harpa davidis variety typical

Left: *Harpa davidis* variety *ventricosa;* right: *Harpa davidis* variety *major*

Living *Harpa crenata.*
Alex Kerstitch photo.

Fully extended *Harpa davidis* var. *major.*
Allan Power photo.

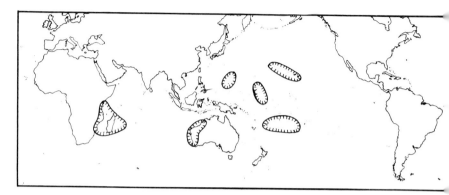

MAP 49. Distribution of *Strombus (Canarium) wilsoni.*

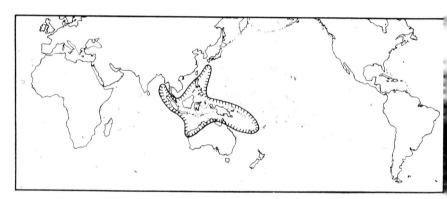

MAP 50. Distribution of *Strombus (Dolomena) dilatatus.*

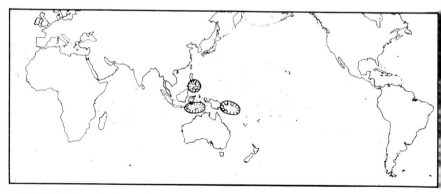

MAP 51. Distribution of *Strombus (Dolomena) kleckhamae.*

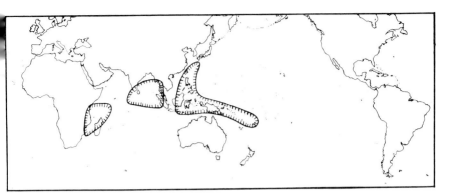

MAP 52. Distribution of *Strombus (Dolomena) labiosus.*

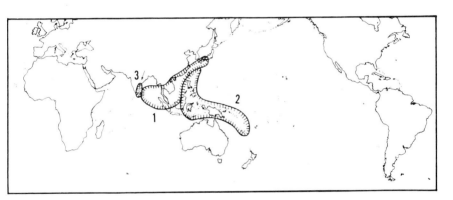

MAP 53. Distribution of *Strombus (Dolomena) marginatus:* 1) *S. m. marginatus;* 2) *S. m. septimus;* 3) *S. m. succinctus.*

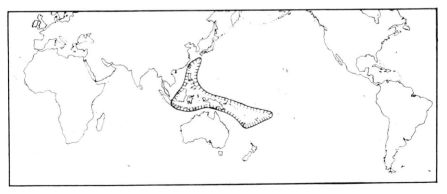

MAP 54. Distribution of *Strombus (Dolomena) minimus.*

161

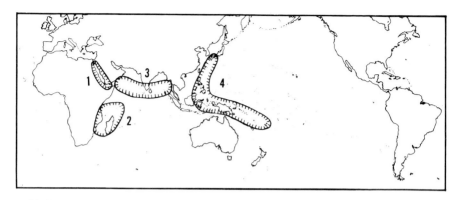

MAP 55. Distribution of *Strombus (Dolomena) plicatus:* 1) *S. p. plicatus;* 2) *S. p. columba;* 3) *S. p. sibbaldi;* 4) *S. p. pulchellus.*

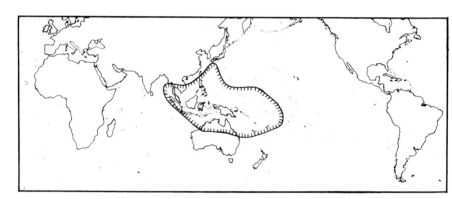

MAP 56. Distribution of *Strombus (Dolomena) variabilis.*

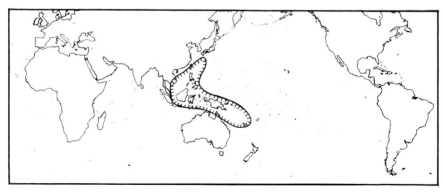

MAP 57. Distribution of *Strombus (Labiostrombus) epidromus.*

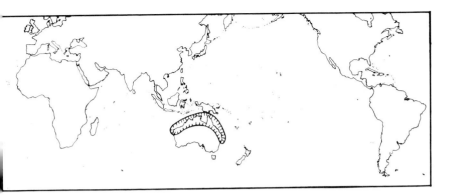

MAP 58. Distribution of *Strombus (Doxander) campbelli.*

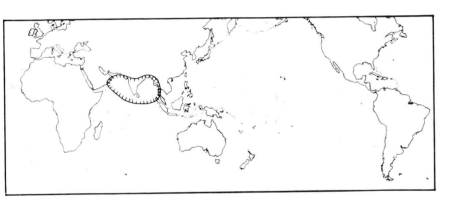

MAP 59. Distribution of *Strombus (Doxander) listeri.*

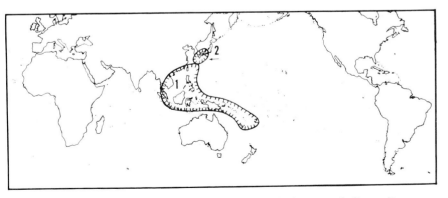

MAP 60. Distribution of *Strombus (Doxander) vittatus:* 1) *S. v. vittatus;* 2) *S. v. japonicus.*

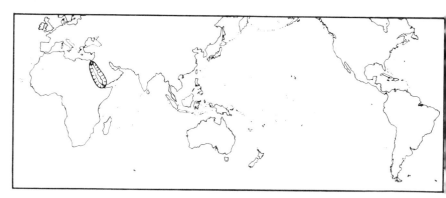

MAP 61. Distribution of *Strombus (Lentigo) fasciatus.*

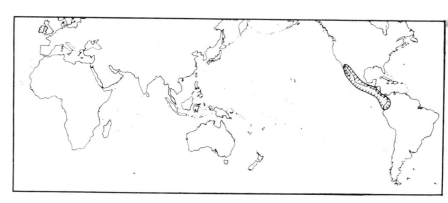

MAP 62. Distribution of *Strombus (Lentigo) granulatus.*

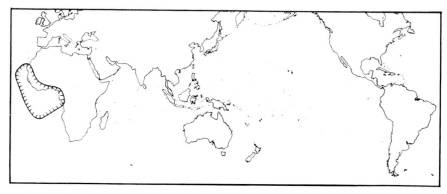

MAP 63. Distribution of *Strombus (Lentigo) latus.*

164

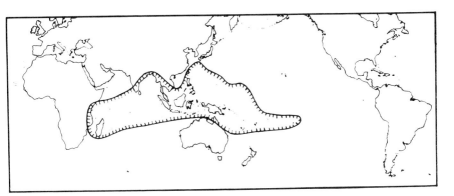

MAP 64. Distribution of *Strombus (Lentigo) lentiginosus.*

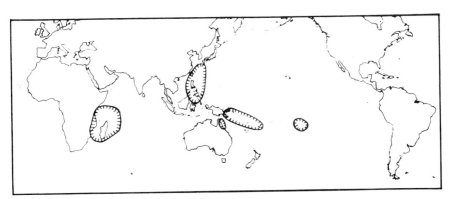

MAP 65. Distribution of *Strombus (Lentigo) pipus.*

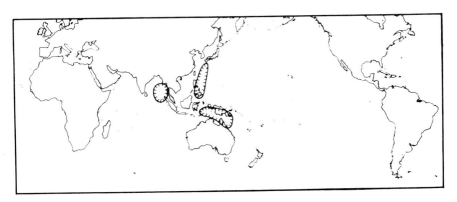

MAP 66. Distribution of *Strombus (Euprotomus) aratrum.*

165

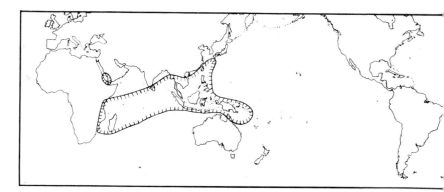

MAP 67. Distribution of *Strombus (Euprotomus) aurisdianae.*

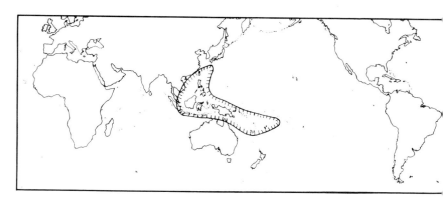

MAP 68. Distribution of *Strombus (Euprotomus) bulla.*

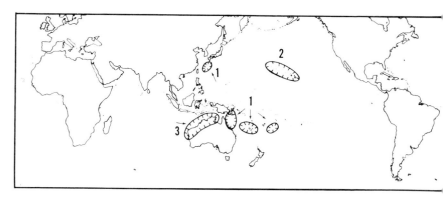

MAP 69. Distribution of *Strombus (Euprotomus) vomer:* 1) *S. v. vomer;* 2) *S. v. hawaiensis;* 3) *S. v. iredalei.*

166

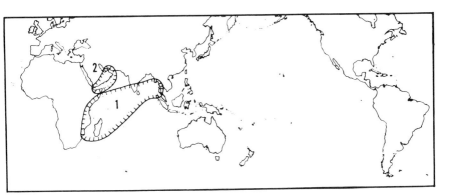

MAP 70. Distribution of *Strombus (Conomurex) decorus:* 1) *S. d. decorus;* 2) *S. d. persicus.*

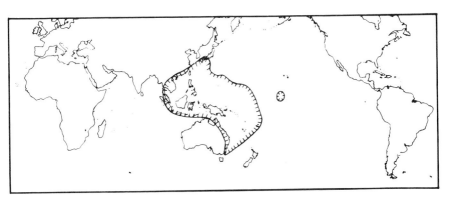

MAP 71. Distribution of *Strombus (Conomurex) luhuanus.*

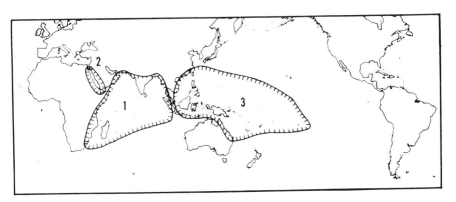

MAP 72. Distribution of *Strombus (Gibberulus) gibberulus:* 1) *S. g. gibberulus;* 2) *S. g. albus;* 3) *S. g. gibbosus.*

167

FAMILY HARPIDAE

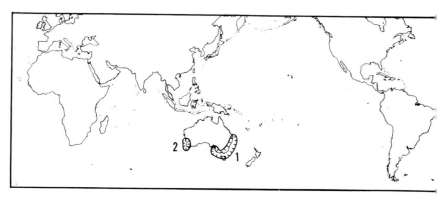

MAP 73. Distribution of *Austroharpa exquisita:* 1) *A. e. exquisita;* 2) *A. e. loisae.*

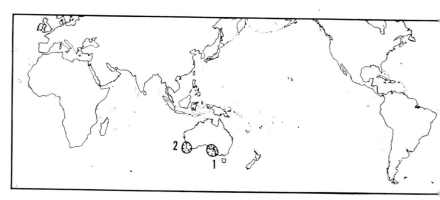

MAP 74. Distribution of *Austroharpa punctata:* 1) *A. p. punctata;* 2) *A. p. wilsoni.*

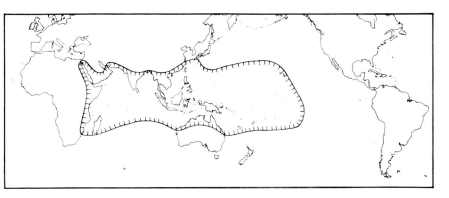

MAP 75. Distribution of *Harpa amouretta.*

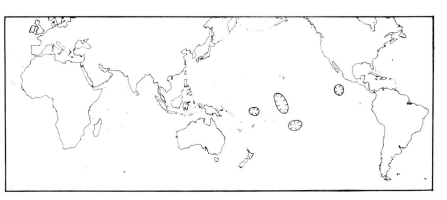

MAP 76. Distribution of *Harpa gracilis.*

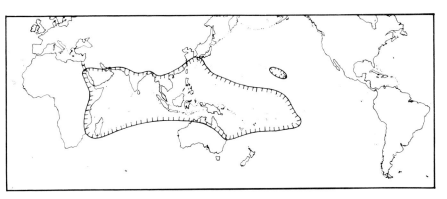

MAP 77. Distribution of *Harpa harpa.*

169

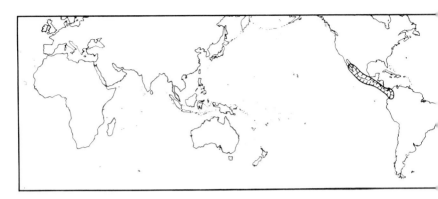

MAP 78. Distribution of *Harpa crenata*.

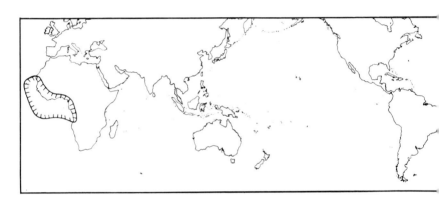

MAP 79. Distribution of *Harpa doris*.

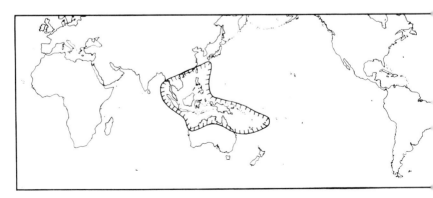

MAP 80. Distribution of *Harpa articularis*.

170

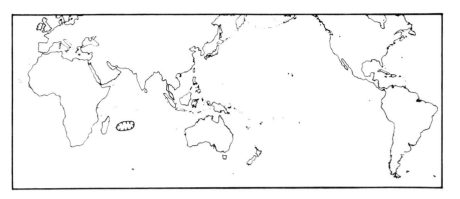

MAP 81. Distribution of *Harpa costata.*

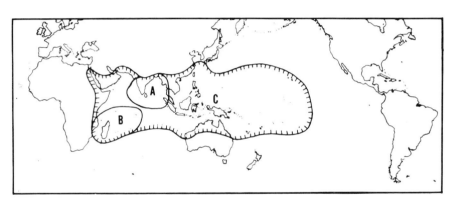

MAP 82. Distribution of *Harpa davidis:* A) var. typical; B) var. *ventricosa;* C) var. *major.*

Family Harpidae

The harps are more advanced molluscs than the conchs, differing radically from them in many characters. They belong to the superfamily Volutacea, along with the volutes, miters, and olives, among others. Like the olives the very large foot of the harp is distinctly divided into two portions, a broad flattened posterior creeping area and an anterior prostomium which is roundly wedged-shaped with distinct corners and a constriction separating it from the rest of the foot. The proboscis is rather small and usually hidden; the eyes are small and located on the outer side of the long tentacles; the siphon is large. The radula is very small and difficult to find in such a large animal. It is poorly known and rarely described, but it appears to consist of only a central tooth with several long cusps; a lateral tooth may be present in the form of a thickened membrane on each side of the central tooth.

Radular teeth of *Harpa amouretta* (left) and *Harpa davidis* var. *major* (after Rehder).

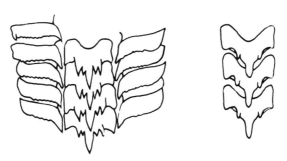

The distinctive shell readily separates harps from olives and all other snails. The species are mostly rather large in size, over 50mm long, with a moderately thin shell structure and a good gloss. The shells of most species are more-or-less covered with ribs that are usually heavy, obvious, and patterned (*Austroharpa* lacks strongly developed ribs and is either smooth or covered with spiral and axial ridges). Between the ribs are usually many fine spiral ridges that are most distinct in juveniles. The anterior end of the shell has a very long columella which is curved, commonly with the ribs forming a sharply scalloped outer margin on the anterior canal. The aperture is very long and wide, the early whorls forming only a small part of the adult shell. Most species have similar color patterns of wavy dark axial lines on a tan to pinkish or yellowish ground color and spiral brownish lines on the ribs.

Sexes are separate in the harps, the male being distinguished by a long, tapering penis coming from the upper right side. There are seemingly no obvious sexual differences in the shells, although it has been suggested that males are more slender. The eggs are laid in batches in tough, translucent, flattened capsules that are wider than high and open by a pore at the dorsal middle margin. In the few recorded clutches there are about ten to twelve capsules laid, each containing about 3,000 to 4,000 very small eggs. The early larval stages are apparently not known, although there is presumably a free-swimming veliger stage. Juveniles are also poorly known and seldom collected.

Harps are mostly deep-water to very deep-water animals, which in part accounts for the poor knowledge of their life history. The *Austroharpa* species are very deep-water, while most *Harpa* species are found in less than 20 meters depth. Only a few *Harpa* species, such as *Harpa amouretta,* are usually found in very shallow water.

Unlike the herbivorous conchs, harps are carnivorous, apparently feeding on small to rather large crabs and shrimps. It has been suggested that the saliva has a quietening effect on the prey, but this is purely speculative.

Genera and Groups of Harpidae

Unlike the numerous poorly defined conch genera and subgenera, the ten species of harps fall into only two fairly distinct genera with no recognizable subgenera. The eight species of *Harpa*, however, can be placed into three rather distinctive groups to aid species identification.

Austroharpa: Small (usually under 30mm long) inflated shells of the southern Australian region; distinct axial ribs are lacking, and the spiral sculpture may be very strong; the protoconch is bulbous and has fewer than three complete whorls. Two species.

Harpa: Usually larger shells (over 30mm) of tropical waters; distinct axial ribs present in all species, the spiral sculpture very weak and inconspicuous in adults; the protoconch has more than three whorls and is relatively smaller and more cylindrical than that of *Austroharpa*. Eight species.

For convenience, the *Harpa* species are placed in three groups:

Group A: Rather small, 20-75 mm long; ribs with clusters of narrow dark lines as the pattern; ventral blotches absent or well developed but seldom or never fused. (*H. amouretta,* etc.)

Group B: Axial dashed lines present alongside and paralleling the ribs; secondary spines commonly present on the posterior part of the ribs. *(H. crenata,* etc.)

Group C: Larger species, commonly over 80mm long; ribs with variable patterns but not clusters of narrow lines or paralleling dashes; strong tendency for ventral blotches to fuse. (*H. articularis,* etc.)

Opposite page: Diagrams of ventral patterns of eight species of *Harpa*.

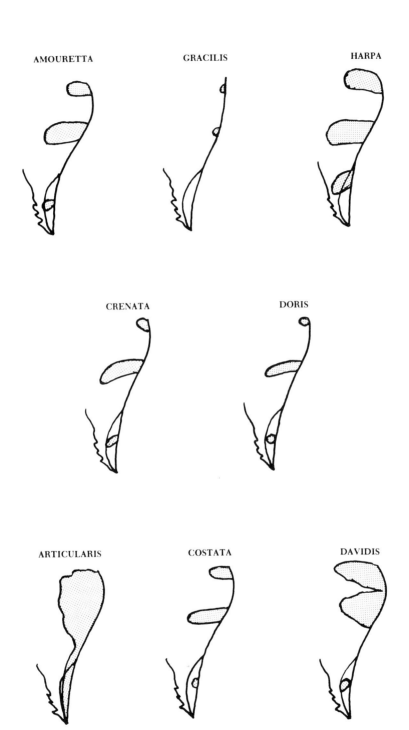

AMOURETTA   GRACILIS   HARPA

CRENATA   DORIS

ARTICULARIS   COSTATA   DAVIDIS

175

Conchs and Harps in the Aquarium

Conchs, specifically *Strombus* and *Lambis,* make excellent additions to the marine aquarium and are in some ways perfect molluscs for display. Many of the species are of moderate size, are rather common in nature, are easily collected, and are apparently fairly hardy in aquariums. As they are herbivores, there is little feeding problem. Conchs will graze on algae growing on stones and the side of the tank as well as on bits of vegetation. They are seldom quarrelsome or aggressive and will only occasionally "cross the line" to become predators on smaller molluscs or crustaceans.

Additionally, conchs are simply interesting animals with a distinct personality. The long eyestalks with gaily colored eyes are in constant searching motion, looking for predators. Only few species burrow in the bottom so strongly as to become invisible. All prefer dark or at least dim surroundings, so probably illumination of the aquarium by red light would allow them to be easily observed at night. It seems rather astounding, but even a rather large conch like *Strombus vomer hawaiensis* is able to ascend vertical glass walls while feeding, so a cover should definitely be used. Spider conchs and some other species "gallop" at a rather rapid rate by using the large operculum somewhat like a mountain climber's pick to pull themselves along.

It is not uncommon for subadult conchs to reach full maturity in the aquarium if properly fed, and it is not impossible to rear conchs from egg strings in the aquarium also. The main problem here is that sufficient planktonic algae of some type must be present to feed the veliger larvae for the two or three weeks before they metamorphose and can use algae growing on the bottom and sides. However, an increasingly large number of commercial algal colonies are available to hobbyists and eventually the problem of raising veligers may be readily solved. Certainly raising experiments indicate the veligers of conchs are not especially sensitive to crowding or wastes as long as they are well fed.

Conditions in the aquarium should be like that for many other marine snails. Full-strength saltwater is required, as is a deep layer of sand or fine gravel for burrowing. The daytime light intensity must be strong enough to allow algae to grow abundantly.

One thing about conchs in the aquarium—avoid predators. Watch out for such things as textile cones, cymatiums, crabs of any type (including hermits), and fish with heavy teeth. Also, for best results do not pair conchs with sea urchins. They will compete for food, and urchins are more aggressive than conchs under most circumstances.

What has been said above applies only to *Strombus* and *Lambis*, which are free-living herbivores. Both the other genera, however, would appear to be detritus feeders, *Terebellum* in shallow water and *Tibia* in deep water. Although common, *Terebellum* is poorly known and apparently spends its active hours buried in the sand. *Tibia* is very poorly known in the living state, but the few references indicate that it is extremely light sensitive. Probably neither genus will do well in aquariums.

Harps are poorly studied, and if they could be successfully kept in the aquarium perhaps it could be more clearly understood how they feed and reproduce. Except for the shallow-water *Harpa amouretta*, few of the harps do well in captivity. If the opportunity arises, try feeding them crabs and fresh shrimp. When threatened, harps, like some olives and related snails, can voluntarily break off the posterior part of their foot, a process known as autotomy. This action is likely to be displayed in the aquarium as it probably serves as a decoy for the "predator" (in this case the aquarist) and gives the harp a few extra seconds to escape.

Collecting Conchs and Harps

Gathering a good collection of conchs and harps is not difficult, although both families have their share of minor rarities and a few very expensive shells. Conchs are especially diverse in price structure, with most of the species available for under five dollars, a few species in the $15-50 range, and a very few species (*S. oldi*, live-taken *S. kleckhamae*, *S. goliath*, *S. vomer hawaiensis*, *Lambis violacea*, and *L. crocatus pilsbryi*) costing $100 or more. Even though most of the rare species of conchs are relatively easy to obtain, the collector will experience difficulty with several of the small species of *Strombus* having restricted ranges. Although apparently not uncommon, such species as *Strombus rugosus*, *S. wilsoni*, *S. microurceus*, and *S. klineorum* are extremely hard to find for sale, perhaps because many dealers have found these species difficult to identify until now. Strombidae is one of the very few collectable families that can be completed by a persistent collector of moderate means, although it may take several years to get the last few species. There are no known species that could be considered extreme rarities on a par with *Conus cervus* or *Cypraea leucodon*.

Harps are a more difficult group to collect although only ten full species are recognized here. Of the eight species of *Harpa*, five are easily available for under $5, *Harpa doris* costs about $60, *Harpa gracilis* is available in the $100 price range, and *Harpa costata* may cost between $300 and $500. *H. costata* is much easier to obtain than *H. gracilis*, however. The real problem with harps is the austroharps, the smallest yet most expensive species and true major rarities. Only *Austroharpa exquisita exquisita* may be obtained for about $300, the other species and subspecies costing $500-800 or so.

Storage of conchs and harps presents more of a problem than in, for instance, cones or cowries because of the great disparity in size of the various species. The average conch or harp can be easily kept in the type of trays and drawers recommended in *Cowries* (Walls, 1979), but the large conchs and spider conchs may easily exceed 150mm in length and often be of equal breadth. They must be kept either in very large drawers or on open shelves (watch out for dust!).

Condition in conchs is on the average not as good as in cowries or even in cones. Adult specimens of conchs can usually be recognized by the thickened lip and often brighter color of the mouth. Adults are more collectable than subadults, given a choice, but there are several factors that may limit the availability of a species to subadults. Full adults may be quite rare while subadults are not uncommon, or full adults may be too worn and disfigured to be considered collectable. Many adults accumulate calcium deposits and barnacles or slipper shells with age, while the thick lip suffers from many small cracks and flaws. Full adults may also develop a thick colored callus over the ventral surface and lip, the callus obscuring the pattern. Large *Lambis* seldom have digits in perfect condition, but subadults have digits that are still open ventrally, a definite sign of immaturity. For the hard-to-get little species almost anything is acceptable, whether eroded beach specimens or covered with calcium crud. Some species, such as *S. klineorum,* are almost always eroded—gems must exist, but if so they are exceedingly rare.

Harps are generally in decent condition, although they are subject to some wear and to growth marks paralleling the ribs. In the common species condition matters little to most dealers and collectors, but with such species as *H. costata* every broken rib counts.

GRADING

Several systems of grading are in use at the moment, the most familiar being the Hawaian Malacological Society HSN-ISGS. This system has severe problems, however, and I personally prefer the simpler Morrison Galleries system. The HSN-ISGS system is presented in *Cowries* (Walls, T.F.H.); the Morrison system follows:

GEM—A mature shell with no noticeable flaws.

FINE—A minor flaw or flaws which do not detract significantly from appearance; shell may be slightly subadult but this will be noted.

GOOD—A noticeable flaw or flaws, or some wear or fading.

FAIR—A shell with significant damage and/or substantial wear.

Plus and minus symbols are used to indicate slightly higher or lower conditions.

Selected Bibliography

The following references have been selected for their basic usefulness and/or availability to collectors. The works by Abbott, Brownell, Clench, and Rehder contain secondary bibliographies that will lead to many earlier but very useful references. The *La Conchiglia* articles are interesting for their large number of illustrations, though they commonly are rather unorthodox treatments of the groups. Strictly systematic literature has not been listed unless it serves to update broader revisionary papers.

Abbott, R.T. 1960. "The genus *Strombus* in the Indo-Pacific," *Indo-Pacific Mollusca*, 1(2): 33-146.

———. 1961. "The genus *Lambis* in the Indo-Pacific," *Indo-Pacific Mollusca*, 1(3): 147-174.

———. 1967. "*Strombus (Canarium) wilsoni* new species from the Indo-Pacific," *Indo-Pacific Mollusca*, 1(7): 455-456.

Brownell, W.N. 1977. "Reproduction and growth of *Strombus gigas, S. costatus* and *S. pugilus* in Los Roques, Venezuela," *Bull. Mar. Sci.*, 27(4): 668-680.

Cernohorsky, W.O. 1971. "New molluscan species of *Strombus* (Strombidae) and *Cancilla* (Mitridae) from New Britain and Taiwan," *Rec. Auckland Inst. Mus.*, 8: 131-135. *(S. kleckhamae)*

Clench, W.J. and R.T. Abbott. 1941. "The genus *Strombus* in the western Atlantic," *Johnsonia*, 1: 1-15. (outdated)

Donati, G. 1969. "Il genere *Aporrhais (= Chenopus)* Da Costa, 1778," *La Conchiglia*, 1(5-6): 10.

Emerson, W.K. 1965. "*Strombus (Tricornis) oldi* new species," *Indo-Pacific Mollusca*, 1(6): 397-398.

Gary, N.A. 1974-1975. "The genus *Lambis* Roeding, 1798," *La Conchiglia*, 4 parts. I - 6(69-70): 3-9; II - 7(71-72): 14-19; III - 7(73-74): 6-9; IV - 7(75-76): 8-9.

Greene, J. 1978. "A new species of *Lambis,*" *La Conchiglia*, 10 (110-111): 11. *(L. wheelwrighti)*

Jung, P. and R.T. Abbott. 1967. "The genus *Terebellum,*" *Indo-Pacific Mollusca*, 1(7): 445-454.

Mallory, G. 1977-1978. "Xenophoridae," *La Conchiglia*, 5 parts. I - 9(101): 3-5; II - 9(102-103): 7-10; III - 10(106-107): 3-6; IV - 10(112-113): 9-10; V - 10(116-117): 4-5.

Mari, A. 1972. "Notes on the genus *Aporrhais*," *La Conchiglia*, 4(43-44): 6-7.

Mienis, H.K. 1969. "Notes on the distribution and morphology of the *Strombus terebellatus*—complex," *Basteria*, 33(5-6): 109-114.

_____ . 1971. "Revision of *Strombus (Canarium) mutabilis ochroglottis* Abbott," *Arch. Moll.*, 101(5/6): 301-304. (*ochroglottis* as full species)

Rehder, H.A. 1973. "The family Harpidae of the world," *Indo-Pacific Mollusca*, 3(16): 207-274.

Romagna-Manoja, E. 1973-1977. "Superfamily Strombacea," *La Conchiglia*, 5 parts. I - 5(57-58): 11-20; II - 6(65-66): 3-13; III - 8(83-84): 3-13; IV - 9(95-96): 3-13; IVa - 9(102-103): 1, 3-4. Also: 1979, 12(130-131): 12-16, 18.

_____ . 1979. "Familia Struthiolariidae Lamarck, 1816," *La Conchiglia*, 11(122-123): 5-7.

Walls, J.G. 1977. "A sorting key to the *Harpa*," *Hawaiian Shell News*, 25(6): 3-4.

_____ . 1978. "Another viewpoint on the living harps," *The Pariah*, # 4: 1-4.

_____ . 1979. *Cowries* (Second Edition). T.F.H. Publ. Inc.; Neptune, N.J.

181

Checklist and Pricing Guide to the Conchs, Tibias, and Harps (1980)

The following prices reflect current price ranges for the various species, subspecies, and some varieties at the time of publication. Generally, lower prices refer to material from localities where the shells are collected in some quantity, while higher prices refer to specimens from unusual localities or of exceptional quality. Unusual colors, lack of roughness of lips or backs, highly developed spines, and degree of maturity all affect prices of conchs and should be taken into consideration when purchasing specimens. In some cases specimens are selling for much higher prices than their actual scarcity would seem to permit; this may be due to simple market fluctuations, scarcity of collectors in the range of the species, or absence of specimen-quality shells on the collector market. Very unstable prices have been indicated by an asterisk (*). As always, the best indicator of prices is a current listing put out by a reputable dealer. Neither the author nor the publisher offers shells for sale; this listing is purely a guide to relative values and not an offer to buy or sell. NP = not priced.

LAMBIS

____ chiragra - $3.-6.
 arthritica - $2.-4.
 rugosa - $5.-8.
____ crocata - $3.-6.
 pilsbryi - $90.-120.
____ digitata - $15.-25.
 crocea - $20.-30.
____ lambis - $1.50-3.

____ millepeda - $1.50-3.
 wheelwrighti -$45.-75.*
____ robusta - $70.-90.
____ scorpius - $1.50-3.
 indomaris - $2.-4.
____ truncata - $10.-20.*
 sebae - $4.-6.
____ violacea - $120.-175.

STROMBUS

____ alatus - $1.-3.
____ aratrum - $3.-6.
 chrysostomus -$20.-40.*
____ aurisdianae - $.50-1.
____ bulla - $1.-2.
____ campbelli - $1.-2.
____ canarium - $.50-1.
 turturella - $.50-1.50
 Albino - $5.-10.
____ costatus - $3.-5.

____ decorus - $1.-2.
 persicus - $1.50-3.
____ dentatus - $1.-3.
____ dilatatus - $1.50-3.
 orosminus -$1.50-2.50
 swainsoni - NP
____ epidromis - $1.-3.
____ erythrinus - $2.-6.
____ fasciatus - $.50-1.50
 Colors - $2.-4.

___ fragilis - $6.-12.
___ fusiformis - $3.-6.
___ galeatus - $5.-8.
___ gallus - $6.-15.
___ gibberulus - $1.50-3.
    albus - $1.-2.
    gibbosus - $.50-1.
___ gigas - $5.-10.
___ goliath - $150.-250.*
___ gracilior - $1.-2.
___ granulatus - $1.-2.
___ haemastoma -$75.-100.
    Mauritius - $50.-75.
___ helli - $15.-30.
___ kleckhamae -$70.-90.*
    Dead - $5.-10.
___ klineorum - $4.-6.
___ labiatus - $.50-1.
    olydius - $2.-5.
___ labiosus - $2.-4.
___ latissimus - $6.-10.
___ latus - $7.-15.
___ lentiginosus -$.50-1.
___ listeri - $10.-20.
___ luhuanus - $.50-1.
___ maculatus - $.50-1.
    depauperatus -$1.-3.
    Hawaii - $2.-4.
___ marginatus - $1.-3.
    septimus - $2.-4.
    succinctus -$1.50.-2.50
___ microurceus - $3.-5.
___ minimus - $1.-2.

___ mutabilis - $.50-2.
    ochroglottus - $1.-2.
    zebriolatus - $2.-5.
___ oldi - $200.-300.
    Dead - $75.-125.
___ peruvianus - $4.-8.
___ pipus - $1.-3.
___ plicatus - $25.-50.*
    columba - $3.-6.
    pulchellus - $4.-6.
    sibbaldi - $7.-10.
___ pugilis - $1.-3.
___ raninus - $1.-3.
___ rugosus - $10.-15.
___ sinuatus - $2.-4.
___ taurus - $35.-50.
    Dead - $5.-10.
___ terebellatus - $3.-5.
    afrobellatus -$10.-15.
___ thersites - $25.-45.
___ tricornis - $5.-12.
___ urceus - $.50-1.
    ustulatus - $.75-2.
    incisus - $2.-3.
    orrae - $.50-1.50
___ variabilis - $1.-2.
    athenius - $1.50-3.
___ vittatus - $1.-3.
    japonicus - $1.50-3.
___ vomer - $15.-25.
    iredalei - $5.-7.
    hawaiensis -$75.-125.*
___ wilsoni - $30.-60.*

TEREBELLUM
___ terebellum - $1.-2.
    Colors - $2.-5.

TIBIA

_____ cancellata - $3.-5.
_____ crispata - $3.-5.
_____ delicatula - $25.-40.
     nana - $6.-10.
_____ fusus - $12.-20.
     melanocheilus -$15.-25.

_____ insulaechorab -$3.-5.
     curta - $4.-8.
     luteostoma -$10.-15.
_____ martini - $10.-20.
     Thin form - $5.-8.
_____ powisi - $2.-4.
     Smooth form -$10.-20.

AUSTROHARPA

_____ exquisita -$300.-400.
     loisae - $500.-750.*

_____ punctata - $400.-600.
     wilsoni - $600.-850.*

HARPA

_____ amouretta - $.50-1.
     Thick form -$1.-1.50
_____ articularis - $2.-3.
_____ costata - $300.-450.*
     Flaws - $150.-200.
_____ crenata - $1.50-3.

_____ davidis - $1.50-3.
     major - $1.50-2.
     ventricosa - $2.-5.
_____ doris - $40.-60.*
     Thick form -$50.-75.
_____ gracilis - $75.-100.
_____ harpa - $2.-3.
     kajiyamai - $50.-75.*

MAP AND COLOR ILLUSTRATION INDEX

Map numbers are indicated in parentheses ( ) preceding the page number of the color illustrations. Only full species are listed.

185

SYNONYMIC INDEX

The following list of Recent strombid and harp names is based mostly on the revisions of the genera by Abbott and Rehder, plus a moderately thorough review of more recent literature. *Tibia* has not been revised recently, so the nomenclature is confused and the relationships of the generic-level taxa are uncertain because of the numerous fossil taxa. This listing is as complete as I could make it through the end of 1979, but certainly some names have been missed. Generic synonyms are listed first under each genus, with subgenera listed as though synonymous with the parent genus. All specific-level names are then listed by genus, with the author and date, followed by an indication of the present allocation of the name. For valid species, the first page of color illustrations in this book is given. Subspecies and varieties are treated as synonyms and not given separate page number references. A question mark indicates doubtful placement.

FAMILY STROMBIDAE

Genus *LAMBIS* Roeding 1798
Harpago Moerch 1852
Heptadactylus Moerch 1852
Millepes Moerch 1852
Millipes Adams & Adams 1854
Pterocera Lamarck 1799
Pteroceras Link 1807
Pteroceres Montfort 1810

aculeatus Perry 1811 = crocata
arachnoides Shikama 1971 = ?
   millepeda x truncata
arthritica Roeding 1798 = chiragra
aurantia Lamarck 1822 = crocata
aurantiacum Sowerby 1825 = crocata
bengalina Grateloup 1840 = truncata
bryonia Gmelin 1791 = truncata
camelus Gray 1826 = lambis
cerea Roeding 1798 = lambis
CHIRAGRA Linnaeus 1758 = valid, 71
CROCATA Link 1807 = valid, 58
crocea Reeve 1842 = crocata
davilae Roeding 1798 = truncata
DIGITATA Perry 1811 = valid, 63

elongata Swainson 1821 = digitata
harpago Roeding 1798 = chiragra
hermaphrodita Roeding 1798 = lambis
indomaris Abbott 1961 = scorpius
kochii Freyer 1855 = chiragra
lacinata Roeding 1798 = lambis
LAMBIS Linnaeus 1758 = valid, 62
lamboides Roeding 1798 = lambis
lobata Roeding 1798 = lambis
maculata Roeding 1798 = lambis
MILLEPEDA Linnaeus 1758 = valid, 63
multipes Sowerby 1842 = violacea
nodosa Lamarck 1816 = scorpius
novemdactylis Deshayes 1843 = digitata
pseudoscorpio Lamarck 1822 = robusta
pseudoscorpio Schubart & Wagner 1829
   = scorpius
radix Roeding 1798 = truncata
radixbryoniae Moerch 1852 = truncata
ROBUSTA Swainson 1821 = valid, 66
rugosum Sowerby 1842 = chiragra
scorpio Murray 1771 = scorpius
SCORPIUS Linnaeus 1758 = valid, 67
sebae Kiener 1843 = truncata
sinuatus Perry 1811 = scorpius

sowerbyi Moerch 1872 = truncata
TRUNCATA Humphrey 1786 =
   valid, 59
undulata Roeding 1798 = ? chiragra
VIOLACEA Swainson 1821 = valid, 70
wheelwrighti Greene 1978 = ?
   millepeda x truncata

Genus *STROMBUS* Linnaeus 1758
Aliger Thiele 1929
Canarium Schumacher 1817
Conomurex Fischer 1884
Conorium Jousseaume 1888
Dolomena Iredale 1931
Doxander Iredale 1931
Euprotomus Gill 1870
Eustrombus Wenz 1940
Gallinula Moerch 1852
Gibberulus Jousseaume 1888
Labiostrombus Oostingh 1925
Laevistrombus Kira 1955
Lentigo Jousseaume 1886
Lobatus Iredale 1921
Monodactylus Moerch 1852
Strombella Schlueter 1838
Strombidea Swainson 1840
Tricornis Jousseaume 1886

accipitrinus Lamarck 1822 = costatus
acutus Perry 1811 = vomer
adansoni Defrance 1827 = latus
adusta Dillwyn 1817 = aratrum
adustus Reeve 1851 = pipus
afrobellatus Abbott 1960 = terebellatus
alata Schumacher 1817 = latissimus
ALATUS Gmelin 1791 = valid, 74
albus Moerch 1850 = gibberulus
anatellus Duclos 1844 = urceus
ARATRUM Roeding 1798 = valid, 135
athenius Duclos 1844 = variabilis
auratus Spalowsky 1795 = latus
AURISDIANAE Linnaeus 1758 =
   valid, 135
australis Schroeter 1805 = vittatus
australis Gray 1826 = vomer
beluchiensis Melvill 1901 = decorus
belutschiensis Melvill 1898 = decorus
bituberculata Lamarck 1822 = raninus
bubo Deshayes 1833 = latus
bubonius Lamarck 1822 = latus
bulbulus Sowerby 1842 = fragilis

BULLA Roeding 1798 = valid, 138
buris Roeding 1798 = aurisdianae
CAMPBELLI Griffith & Pidgeon 1834
   = valid, 126
canaliculatus Burry 1949 = gigas
CANARIUM Linnaeus 1758 = valid, 75
cancellatus Pease 1860 = helli
carinata Roeding 1798 = marginata
carnaria Roeding 1798 = latus
carnea Roeding 1798 = latus
chemnitzii Pfeiffer 1840 = vomer
chrysostomus Kuroda 1942 = aratrum
columba Lamarck 1822 = plicatus
coniformis Sowerby 1842 = decorus
corrugatus Adams & Reeve 1848 =
   rugosus
COSTATUS Gmelin 1791 = valid, 78
crassilabrum Anton 1839 = ??
   urceus
crenatus Sowerby 1825 = galeatus
cristatus Lamarck 1822 = sinuatus
cylindricus Swainson 1821 = decorus
DECORUS Roeding 1798 = valid, 142
deformis Griffith & Pidgeon 1834
   = plicatus
DENTATUS Linnaeus 1758 = valid, 91
depauperata Dautzenberg &
   Bouge 1933 = maculatus
DILATATUS Swainson 1821 = valid,
   111
dilatatus Lamarck 1822 = latus
donnellyi Iredale 1931 = vomer
dubius Swainson 1823 = ? fragilis
elatus Anton 1839 = ?? vittatus
elegans Sowerby 1842 = erythrinus
elegans Romagna-Manoja 1973 = fasciatus
elegantissima Roeding 1798 =
   fasciatus
EPIDROMIS Linnaeus 1758 = valid,
   126
epimellus Duclos 1844 = mutabilis
ERYTHRINUS Dillwyn 1817 = valid, 91
expansa Tryon 1885 = epidromis
exustus Swainson 1822 = pipus
FASCIATUS Born 1778 = valid, 130
fasciatus Gmelin 1791 = latus
flammea Link 1807 = decorus
flavigula Tryon 1885 = fasciatus
floridus Lamarck 1822 = mutabilis
flosculosus Moerch 1852 = mutabilis

FRAGILIS Roeding 1798 = valid, 94
FUSIFORMIS Sowerby 1842 = valid, 94
galea Wood 1828 = galeatus
GALEATUS Swainson 1823 = valid, 78
GALLUS Linnaeus 1758 = valid, 79
GIBBERULUS Linnaeus 1758 = valid,
   143
gibbosus Roeding 1798 = gibberulus
gibbus Issel & T.-Canefri, 1876 =
   canarium
GIGAS Linnaeus 1758 = valid, 79
GOLIATH Schroeter 1805 = valid, 82
goliath Dillwyn 1817 = goliath
GRACILIOR Sowerby 1825 = valid, 74
GRANULATUS Swainson 1822 =valid,
   131
guttatus Kiener 1843 = bulla
HAEMASTOMA Sowerby 1842 = valid,
   95
hawaiensis Pilsbry 1917 = vomer
HELLI Kiener 1843 = valid, 95
hirasei Kuroda 1942 = vomer
horridus Smith 1940 = gigas
incisus Wood 1828 = urceus
inermis Swainson 1822 = costatus
iredalei Abbott 1960 = vomer
isabella Lamarck 1822 = canarium
ismarius Duclos 1844 = decorus
japonicus Reeve 1851 = vittatus
kieneri Issel & T.-Canefri 1876 = plicatus
KLECKHAMAE Cernohorsky 1971 =
   valid, 114
KLINEORUM Abbott 1960 = valid, 99
LABIATUS Roeding 1798 = valid, 98
labiatus Perry 1811 = gibberulus
LABIOSUS Wood 1828 = valid, 111
labrosus Menke 1829 = ?? luhuanus
laciniatus Dillwyn 1817 = sinuatus
laevilabris Menke 1828 = decorus
laevis Perry 1811 = bulla
laevis Dodge 1946 = urceus
lamarckii Swainson 1840 = bulla
lamarckii Sowerby 1842 = aurisdianae
LATISSIMUS Linnaeus 1758 = valid, 82
LATUS Gmelin 1791 = valid, 131
leidyi Heilprin 1887 = costatus
LENTIGINOSUS Linnaeus 1758 =
   valid, 134
lineatus Lamarck 1822 = fasciatus
lineolatus Wood 1828 = fasciatus
LISTERI Gray 1852 = valid, 130

lituratus Menke 1829 = variabilis
lobata Roeding 1798 = sinuatus
lobatus Lamarck 1822 = raninus
LUHUANUS Linnaeus 1758 = valid, 143
lutruanus Dillwyn 1823 = decorus
MACULATUS Sowerby 1842 = valid, 99
MARGINATUS Linnaeus 1758 = valid,
   115
mauritianus Lamarck 1822 = decorus
melanostomus Sowerby 1825 = aratrum
melastomus Swainson 1822 = aratrum
MICROURCEUS Kira 1959 = valid,
   102
miniata Link 1807 = decorus
MINIMUS Linnaeus 1771 = valid, 119
mirabilis Sowerby 1870 = listeri
muricatus Watson 1885 = urceus
MUTABILIS Swainson 1821 = valid,
   103
nanus Bales 1942 = raninus
nicaraguensis Fluck 1905 = pugilis
novaezelandiae Reeve 1842 = vomer
ochroglottis Abbott 1960 = mutabilis
OLDI Emerson 1965 = valid, 83
olydius Duclos 1844 = labiatus
orientalis Duclos 1844 = tricornis
orosminus Duclos 1844 = dilatatus
orrae Abbott 1960 = urceus
otiolum Iredale 1931 = ? labiatus
pacificus Swainson 1821 = vomer
palmata Fischer 1807 = sinuatus
papilio Dillwyn 1817 = pipus
peculiaris Smith 1940 = pugilis
persicus Swainson 1821 = decorus
pertinax Duclos 1844 = tricornis
PERUVIANUS Swainson 1823 = valid,
   86
picta Roeding 1798 = latissimus
PIPUS Roeding 1798 = valid, 134
PLICATUS Roeding 1798 = valid, 119
plicatus Lamarck 1816 = labiatus
polyfasciatus Dillwyn 1817 = fasciatus
ponderosus Philippi 1842 = thersites
PUGILIS Linnaeus 1758 = valid, 75
pulchellus Reeve 1851 = plicatus
pusillus Anton 1839 = ? luhuanus
radians Duclos 1844 = erythrinus
rana Roeding 1798 = lentiginosus
RANINUS Gmelin 1791 = valid, 86
rarimus Bosc 1801 = raninus
reticulata Link 1807 = ?? urceus

rhodostomus Martens 1869 = gibberulus
robustus Sowerby 1874 = marginatus
RUGOSUS Sowerby 1825 = valid, 102
ruppelli Reeve 1850 = erythrinus
samar Dillwyn 1817 = dentatus + fragilis
samarensis Reeve 1851 = dentatus
samba Clench 1937 = gigas
scalariformis Duclos 1833 = haemastoma
septimus Duclos 1844 = marginatus
sibbaldii Sowerby 1842 = plicatus
SINUATUS Humphrey 1786 = valid, 87
sloani Leach 1814 = pugilis
solitaris Perry 1811 = gallus
spectabilis Verrill 1950 = costatus
stiva Roeding 1798 = aurisdianae
striatogranosus Martens 1880 =
    aurisdianae
subulatus Herbst 1788 = fasciatus
succinctus Linnaeus 1767 = marginatus
sulcata Watson 1886 = campbelli
sulcatus Holten 1802 = ? vittatus
sulcatus Anton 1839 = ?? gracilior
swainsoni Reeve 1850 = dilatatus
taeniatus Quoy & Gaimard 1834 =
    canarium
tankervillii Swainson 1823 = plicatus
TAURUS Reeve 1857 = valid, 87
TEREBELLATUS Sowerby 1842 =
    valid, 106
THERSITES Swainson 1823 = valid, 90
TRICORNIS Humphrey 1786 = valid,
    90
tricornis Fischer 1807 = tricornis
tridentatus Gmelin 1791 = dentatus
troglodytes Lamarck 1822 = minimus
tubercularis Anton 1839 = ?? decorus
turritus Lamarck 1822 = vittatus
turturella Roeding 1798 = canarium
undulatus Kuester 1845 = alatus
URCEUS Linnaeus 1758 = valid, 107
ustulatum Schumacher 1817 = urceus
vanikorensis Quoy & Gaimard 1834 =
    canarium
VARIABILIS Swainson 1820 = valid,
    123
verrilli McGinty 1946 = gigas
VITTATUS Linnaeus 1758 = valid, 127
VOMER Roeding 1798 = valid, 138
WILSONI Abbott 1967 = valid, 110
yerburyi Smith 1891 = plicatus

zebriolata Adams & Leloup 1938
    = mutabilis
zelandiae Gray 1826 = vomer

Genus *TEREBELLUM* Roeding 1798
Artopoia Gistel 1848
Lucis Gistel 1848
Terebrina Rafinesque 1815

album Link 1807 = terebellum
delicatum Kuroda & Kawamoto 1961 =
    terebellum
lineatum Roeding 1798 = terebellum
nebulosum Roeding 1798 = terebellum
punctatum Reeve 1863 = terebellum
punctulorum Roeding 1798 = terebellum
subulatum Lamarck 1811 = terebellum
TEREBELLUM Linnaeus 1758 = valid,
    55
terebra Bosc 1801 = terebellum
variegatum Link 1807 = terebellum

Genus *TIBIA* Roeding 1798
Gladius Adams & Adams 1854
Rimella Agassiz 1841
Rostellaria Lamarck 1799
Rostellariella Thiele 1929
Rostellum Montfort 1810
Varicospira Eames 1952

abyssicola Schepman 1909 = powisi
brevirostris Schumacher 1817 =
    insulaechorab
CANCELLATA Lamarck 1822 = valid,
    54
clavus Gmelin 1791 = fusus
CRISPATA Sowerby 1842 = valid, 54
curta Sowerby 1842 =
    insulaechorab
curvirostris Lamarck 1822 =
    insulaechorab
DELICATULA Nevill 1881 = valid, 47
dentula Perry 1811 = insulaechorab
favanni Pfeiffer 1817 = fusus (serratus)
fissus Dillwyn 1817 = fusus (serratus)
FUSUS Linnaeus 1758 = valid, 47
INSULAECHORAB Roeding 1798 =
    valid, 50
lee Iredale 1958 = cancellata

luteostoma Angas 1878 = insulaechorab
magna Schroeter 1802 = insulaechorab
MARTINI Marrat 1877 = valid, 51
melanocheilus Adams 1854 = fusus
minor Schepman 1909 = cancellata
moretonensis Romagna-Manoja 1977 =
   powisi
nana Romagna-Manoja 1977 = delicatula
POWISI Petit 1840 = valid, 55
serrata Perry 1811 = fusus
sinensis Perry 1811 = fusus
speciosa Adams & Adams 1863 = ?
   crispata
tyleri Adams & Adams 1863 = ?
   cancellata
unicornis Dillwyn 1817 = fusus

FAMILY HARPIDAE

Genus *AUSTROHARPA* Finlay 1931
Palamharpa Iredale 1931

EXQUISITA Iredale 1931 = valid,
   147
loisae Rehder 1973 = exquisita
PUNCTATA Verco 1896 = valid, 147
wilsoni Rehder 1973 = punctata

Genus *HARPA* Roeding 1798
Cithara Jousseaume 1881
Harpalis Link 1807
Harparia Rafinesque 1815

AMOURETTA Roeding 1798 = valid,
   150
ARTICULARIS Lamarck 1822 = valid,
   155
cabritii Fischer 1860 = davidis
cancellata Roeding 1798 = davidis

conoidalis Lamarck 1822 = davidis
COSTATA Linnaeus 1758 = valid, 155
crassa Krauss 1848 = amouretta
CRENATA Swainson 1822 = valid, 154
DAVIDIS Roeding 1798 = valid, 158
delicata Perry 1811 = ?? articularis
DORIS Roeding 1798 = valid, 154
GRACILIS Broderip & Sowerby 1829 =
   valid, 150
grandiformis Perry 1811 = davidis
gruneri Sutor 1877 = costata
HARPA Linnaeus 1758 = valid, 151
harpa Wood 1818 = davidis
imperialis Lamarck 1822 = costata
kajiyamai Habe 1970 = harpa
kajiyamai Rehder 1973 = harpa
kawamurai Habe & Kosuge 1970 =
   not seen
laetifica Melvill 1916 = costata
ligata Menke 1828 = davidis
major Roeding 1798 = davidis
minor Lamarck 1822 = amouretta
multicostata Sowerby 1822 = costata
nablium Moerch 1852 = davidis
nobilis Roeding 1798 = harpa
nobilis Lamarck 1816 = articularis
oblonga Schumacher 1817 = amouretta
rivoliana Lesson 1834 = crenata
rosea Lamarck 1816 = doris
rosea Kiener 1835 = crenata
scriba Valenciennes 1832 = crenata
solidula Adams 1854 = amouretta
striata Lamarck 1816 = davidis
striatula Adams 1854 = davidis
testudo Donovan 1822 = davidis
ventricosa Lamarck 1822 = davidis
virginalis Sowerby 1870 = amouretta
vulgaris Schumacher 1817 = davidis